Checklist for Life
for teens

Presented To:

_____

Presented By:

_____

Date:

_____

Checklist for Life

for teens

Checklist for Life
for teens

THOMAS NELSON PUBLISHERS®
Nashville

A Division of Thomas Nelson, Inc.
www.ThomasNelson.com

Managing Editor: Lila Empson
Manuscript written and prepared by Marcia Ford
Teen Consultant: Amanda Corn
Design: Whisner Design Group

Checklist for life for teens
    p. cm.
ISBN 0-7852-6461-2 (pbk.)
1. Christian teenagers–Religious life. I. Thomas Nelson Publishers.
BV4531.3.C48 2002
248.8'3—dc21
                    2002006086

Printed in the United States of America

04 05 06   CJK   12 11 10 09

Heart Attitude

I will honor God with my life.

Table of Contents

Table of Contents Continued

Introduction

You are standing on the brink of adulthood, the wide, open spaces of your future spread out before you the way the American West must have looked to the early explorers. The possibilities seem endless and exciting. Others crossed the land before, however, and sent back reports of treacherous mountain passes and spooky canyons, blinding blizzards and tormenting droughts, venomous rattlers and ravenous grizzlies. The breathtaking views from the "purple mountains' majesty" weren't as appealing in fact as they were in imagination.

Take heart. There are safe passages over the land you are about to enter. You can learn to find those passages by preparing yourself in advance, starting right now. What is even better is that you won't have to wait five or ten or twenty years for the payoff, because the discoveries you make will benefit you today, as well as in the future.

This book, like others in the Checklist for Life series, is designed to encourage you on your journey by drawing on the wisdom found in the ultimate travel guide, the

Bible—so keep your Bible nearby. Each overview or insight passage stands alone and focuses on a specific theme. The way you use this book is up to you, working through the book in sequence or reading the entries on specific topics in order of their relevance to your life today. After each passage, reflect on the I Will checklist and perform the actions in the Things to Do checklist. You'll be asked to write some of your thoughts in a journal, so keep a notebook—any kind will do—with your Bible.

Get everything together for your journey: a Bible, a notebook and pen, *Checklist for Life for Teens*, and an open mind and heart. Before you set out, invite God's Spirit to lead you every step of the way. You now have all the equipment you need to get started. Enjoy the journey!

You are not a human being in search of a spiritual experience.
You are a spiritual being immersed in a human experience.
—PIERRE TEILHARD DE CHARDIN

God is the friend of silence. See how nature—trees, flowers, grass—grow in silence? The more we receive in silent prayer, the more we can give in our active life.

—MOTHER TERESA

Everybody can be great. Because anybody can serve... You only need a heart full of grace. A soul generated by love.

—MARTIN LUTHER KING

Let no one despise your youth, but be an example to the believers in word, in conduct, in love, in spirit, in faith, in purity.

1 TIMOTHY 4:12 NKJV

God does not love us because we are valuable. We are valuable because God loves us.

MARTIN LUTHER

I will praise You, for I am fearfully and wonderfully made; marvelous are Your works, and that my soul knows very well.

PSALM 139:14 NKJV

Let us treat men and women well; treat them as if they were real. Perhaps they are.

RALPH WALDO EMERSON

Your ears shall hear a word behind you, saying, "This is the way, walk in it," whenever you turn to the right hand or whenever you turn to the left.

ISAIAH 30:21 NKJV

A loving heart is the truest wisdom.

CHARLES DICKENS

Checklist for Life for teens

The art of contentment is the recognition that the most satisfying and the most dependably refreshing experiences of life lie not in great things but in little.
        —Edgar Andrew Collard

I know the thoughts that I think toward you, says the LORD, thoughts of peace and not of evil, to give you a future and a hope.
        —Jeremiah 29:11 NKJV

Mirror, Mirror

I will praise You, for I am fearfully and wonderfully made; marvelous are Your works, and that my soul knows very well.

—Psalm 139:14 NKJV

You are made in the image of God. Hard to believe? You know what it's like to look in the mirror and groan at what you see. Sometimes, the longer you look, the worse it gets! It doesn't help much when your parents tell you that you're just going through a phase, that even the best-looking kids in school think they're ugly or dorky or homely. You see every one of your flaws as clearly as if a huge neon arrow was pointing right at them.

In a way, mirrors distort your true image, especially when you've trained your eyes to see flaws that aren't even there. It's almost as if you're looking into the wavy mirrors in a funhouse—they pull your body this way and that, squish your features, and turn you into a hideous alien from some remote planet. What you need to do is train your eyes to focus on the incredibly wonderful work of God that's staring back at you.

What you think are flaws are often features that simply differ from those of the celebrities you see on television and movie screens and billboards and magazine covers. Are those images typical of reality? No. All you have to do is look around you for one day to realize how few people fit that ideal image. Not everyone can—or, believe it, wants to—look like Mandy Moore or Josh Harnett. That's a good thing. Think how monotonous and confusing life would be otherwise.

It's the truth: You are made in the image of God, and He has a never-ending supply of features to draw from. He designed every individual in a unique way, right down to the tiniest detail. You can either get mad at God for that, or you can be grateful to Him for caring so much about the way you turned out. Who else has paid you that much attention? Even if anyone else wanted to, no one else could.

In fact, God seems to enjoy lavishing His attention on those who seldom get any. By today's standards, Jeremiah was just a kid when God singled him out to be His spokesman. When Jeremiah objected and pointed out all his flaws, God basically told him to chill. David seems to have been the runt of his family's litter, and he ended up a king. And one Old Testament reference to the Messiah even implies that He—Jesus, that is—wasn't much to look at.

Instead of obsessing over your image in the mirror, try mirroring the image of Jesus, the one that reflects His character. How would you look if you were compassionate toward others and if you went out of your way to help your parents, showed kindness to your siblings, and treated everyone equally—even the misfits at your school? You'd start to feel pretty good about yourself, and the way you feel about yourself on the inside always shows up on your face.

Just for today, try thinking about yourself as a new creation. Turn the Golden Rule back on yourself: Do unto yourself as you would have others do unto you! Be good to yourself by refusing to think that you're anything less than terrific. Surround yourself with those friends that make you feel special and significant. Don't even try on the victim role. Laugh right out loud when the mirror tries to tell you you're not the fairest—or handsomest—one of all.

Does all this sound vain? Aren't you supposed to not think all that highly of yourself? Few teenagers, way down deep inside, have a problem with an inflated self-esteem. What the Bible says is that you should not think any more highly of yourself than you ought to. In other words, you need to have an honest, undistorted image of who you are—a unique and cherished person created by the highly creative God. No more than that, of course, but certainly no less than that as well.

Before you were born, God dipped His hand into His limitless well of resources and came up with the precise components He wanted to use to create you. Mirrors do lie, each time they tell you that you're anything less than the very best God has to offer.

I Will

Believe that I am wonderfully made.   *yes*   *no*
_____   _____

Be thankful for the unique features God has given me.   *yes*   *no*
_____   _____

Base my self-image on the image of God.   *yes*   *no*
_____   _____

Surround myself with friends who accept me as I am.   *yes*   *no*
_____   _____

Understand that my friends are also special to God.   *yes*   *no*
_____   _____

Think positive thoughts about myself.   *yes*   *no*
_____   _____

Question negative feedback from my mirror.   *yes*   *no*
_____   _____

Things to Do

☐ Thank God today for the way He made you.

☐ Read Psalm 139 and really think about what it says.

☐ Make a list of your good features. Ask a trusted friend to add to the list.

☐ Catch yourself doing something right today—and smile about it.

☐ Look in the mirror and tell yourself that you are made in the image of God.

☐ Ask God to show you how you can accept yourself completely.

Things to Remember

The Lord said to Samuel, "Do not look at his appearance or at his physical stature, because I have refused him. For the Lord does not see as man sees; for man looks at the outward appearance, but the Lord looks at the heart."

1 SAMUEL 16:7 NKJV

If any man is in Christ, he is a new creature; the old things passed way; behold, new things have come.

2 CORINTHIANS 5:17 NASB

To the praise of the glory of His grace, by which He made us accepted in the Beloved.

—EPHESIANS 1:6 NKJV

Do not judge according to appearance, but judge with righteous judgment.

JOHN 7:24 NKJV

Do not let your adornment be merely outward—arranging the hair, wearing gold, or putting on fine apparel—rather let it be the hidden person of the heart, with the incorruptible beauty of a gentle and quiet spirit, which is very precious in the sight of God.

1 PETER 3:3–4 NKJV

Jesus said to him, "'You shall love the Lord your God with all your heart, with all your soul, and with all your mind.' This is the first and great commandment. And the second is like it: 'You shall love your neighbor as yourself.'"

MATTHEW 22:37–39 NKJV

This precious treasure—this light and power that now shine within us—is held in perishable containers, that is, in our weak bodies.

2 CORINTHIANS 4:7 NLT

Your hands have made me and fashioned me; give me understanding, that I may learn Your commandments.

PSALM 119:73 NKJV

Thus says the LORD, your Redeemer, and He who formed you from the womb: "I am the LORD, who makes all things, who stretches out the heavens all alone, who spreads abroad the earth by Myself."

ISAIAH 44:24 NKJV

The LORD gave me a message. He said, "I knew you before I formed you in your mother's womb. Before you were born I set you apart and appointed you as my spokesman to the world." "O Sovereign LORD," I said, "I can't speak for you! I'm too young!"

JEREMIAH 1:4–6 NLT

God does not love us because we are valuable. We are valuable because God loves us.

—MARTIN LUTHER

Nothing is a greater impediment to being on good terms with others than being ill at ease with yourself.

—HONORÉ DE BALZAC

Things Fall Apart

Jesus said, "Come to Me, all you who labor and are heavy laden, and I will give you rest."

—Matthew 11:28 NKJV

Did you know that you can turn any problem over to God and He will help? Maybe your life has gotten so bad that you wish you could change places with somebody else—in fact, just about anybody else. Maybe your dog had to be put to sleep, or you had to move away from all your friends. Maybe your grandmother died. Maybe your mother or father is so immersed in personal problems that you're being ignored. Maybe your coach had to resign because of serious health problems. Any one of these things could turn your world upside down.

Life-changing situations that involve loss can be dangerous if you don't know how to respond to them. Know that you don't have to go through any of these situations by yourself. You can turn them over to God and lean on Him. The first step in a healthy response to trauma is to admit that you're hurting or that you're angry or that you don't feel like going on. Denying your feelings can set

you up for serious disorders—depression, for example—
and prevent you from getting the help you need.

If you find yourself in an emotionally shattering
situation, immediately turn the problem over to God. By
acknowledging that you have no control over the situation
and that there isn't a thing you can do to change it, you
place yourself in the best position possible to truly let go of
it. Allow God and others to help you handle your loss and
make sense of your life again. Find someone willing to listen
as you vent your feelings—a pastor, a counselor, maybe an
aunt or uncle.

A special word of caution if your loss is related to your
parents' divorce or separation: Don't take responsibility for
their decisions. Don't blame yourself. Don't think you can fix
the problem. Do the most important thing you can do:
Continue to love your parents and pray for God's will to be
done. Place their relationship in God's hands and leave it
there.

Dealing with loss is a process for which there is no
instant cure. A particularly devastating loss can take months
or years to recover from, but as you draw closer to God,
you will begin to feel better much sooner. Make sure you
take a few moments each day to focus on what you still
have instead of what you've lost. In time, you will probably
discover that you wouldn't want to trade places with
anyone else.

I Will

Turn to God to see me through this. _____ yes _____ no

Acknowledge that I have no control over the situation. _____ yes _____ no

Be thankful for what I still have. _____ yes _____ no

Admit how much I hurt when things fall apart. _____ yes _____ no

Realize that in time, I will begin to feel better. _____ yes _____ no

Understand that there is no instant cure for getting over a loss. _____ yes _____ no

Things to Do

☐ Ask God to help you handle the loss you've experienced.

☐ Identify what you fear most about the loss you've suffered and give that fear to God.

☐ Read Psalms 16, 23, 130, and 138.

☐ Go through one day fully alert to all the things you still have.

☐ Write down your thoughts and feelings about loss in a journal.

☐ Find someone to talk to.

Things to Remember

Jesus said, "The Spirit of the Lord is upon Me, because He has anointed me to preach the gospel to the poor; He has sent Me to heal the brokenhearted, to proclaim liberty to the captives and recovery of sight to the blind, to set at liberty those who are oppressed."

LUKE 4:18 NKJV

God, who called you to become his child, will do all this for you, just as he promised.

1 THESSALONIANS 5:24 TLB

Because he has set his love upon Me, therefore I will deliver him; I will set him on high, because he has known My name.

PSALM 91:14 NKJV

The angel of the LORD camps around those who fear God, and he saves them.

PSALM 34:7 NCV

LORD, You have been our dwelling place in all generations.

PSALM 90:1 NKJV

While we may not be able to control all that happens to us, we can control what happens inside us.

BENJAMIN FRANKLIN

Nothing that grieves us can be called little: by the eternal laws of proportion a child's loss of a doll and a king's loss of a crown are events of the same size.

MARK TWAIN

Exclusive Offer

---

*So you may walk in the way of goodness, and keep to the
paths of righteousness.*

—Proverbs 2:20 NKJV

Anyone who's been in middle school or high school
for more than a day knows about cliques—those narrow,
exclusive groups of kids who make others feel unwelcome.
If you're one of the many who have been banished from a
clique, you know how awful that can feel. But being
accepted by a clique isn't all it's cracked up to be.

If you're part of a clique now, you need to think
carefully about the choice you've made. Most cliques
create an imaginary circle around their tight little group
and treat everyone outside the circle as if they're diseased.
Someone always gets hurt, and the clique acquires a
reputation for meanness. And if you have identified
yourself with Christ, that's not exactly the kind of
reputation you want to have.

In fact, your identity in Christ should be one of the

most important factors you use in deciding if you really want to be a part of any group. A clique tends to take on a personality of its own and homogenize the personalities of its members. You could lose your individuality. Is that really what you want? You as a Christian are a son or daughter of the King; that's an identity worth hanging on to!

The more certain you are of your identity in Christ, the less need you'll have to find your identity in a clique or in anything else. Try to get a clear picture in your mind of who you are in the family of God: an heir of the kingdom, a person of infinite worth, one in whom God's Spirit lives. You have been bought with a price—Jesus' death on the cross—and you belong to God. Jesus is now your friend and your brother. You are holy and acceptable in God's sight, and He says that nothing can separate you from His love. Pretty heady stuff, but that's exactly what your identity in Christ is all about.

Remember this: God extends His kindness beyond the circle of those who identify with Him; His kindness is never exclusive. Make it your goal to so identify with Christ that your acts of kindness extend to those inside and outside the cliques at your school. With your identity firmly established in Jesus Christ, you'll no doubt find it easier to break down those clique-built barriers, one person at a time.

I Will

Consider my identity in Christ before joining any group.

yes _____ no _____

Get a clear picture in my mind of who I am in Jesus Christ.

yes _____ no _____

Allow God to use me to break down the barriers that cliques have built.

yes _____ no _____

Avoid being part of any group that acts superior to others.

yes _____ no _____

Make others feel welcome in my circle of friends.

yes _____ no _____

Extend kindness to others.

yes _____ no _____

Things to Do

☐ Write "I am child of the King" on a piece of paper and place it in your wallet as a reminder of who you are in Christ.

☐ Ask God to reveal any blind spots you have in the way you treat others and resolve to correct the problem by modeling your behavior after Jesus'.

☐ List specific things you can do to show kindness to those outside your immediate circle of friends.

☐ Identify one person you've judged unfairly and carefully attempt to befriend him or her.

☐ Sit next to someone in the cafeteria that you don't normally eat lunch with.

Things to Remember

The LORD said, "You shall do no injustice in judgment. You shall not be partial to the poor, nor honor the person of the mighty. In righteousness you shall judge your neighbor."

LEVITICUS 19:15 NKJV

God created humans to be like himself; he made men and women.

GENESIS 1:27 CEV

My little children, let us not love in word or in tongue, but in deed and in truth. And by this we know that we are of the truth, and shall assure our hearts before Him. For if our heart condemns us, God is greater than our heart, and knows all things.

1 JOHN 3:18–20 NKJV

Are you doing anything remarkable if you welcome only your friends? Everyone does that!

MATTHEW 5:47 GOD'S WORD

Love the stranger, for you were strangers in the land of Egypt.

DEUTERONOMY 10:19 NKJV

• •

We forfeit three-fourths of ourselves in order to be like other people.

ARTHUR SCHOPENHAUER

Three things in human life are important: The first is to be kind. The second is to be kind. And the third is to be kind.

HENRY JAMES

Loose Lips

A talebearer reveals secrets, but he who is of a faithful spirit conceals a matter.

—*Proverbs 11:13* NKJV

Like many unwed teenage mothers, this one—a girl of about fifteen—had to endure the whispers behind her back. She seemed like such a good girl. Oh well, one never can tell. And I hear the man she's with isn't even the father of the child—no telling who is.

We don't know for sure that all that took place, but knowing human nature, we can probably assume that those were the kinds of things that were said about Mary before she gave birth to Jesus. The facts don't lie, people say: Mary is not married, Mary is pregnant, and Joseph is not the father; therefore, Mary is not the good girl we thought she was. But the gossips didn't have all the facts, did they? It was that one little missing fact—rather, that one huge fact— that made all the difference in the truth of the story.

Nothing good can come of gossip. Gossip—which includes passing along secrets and talking negatively about others—destroys relationships, ruins lives, and causes a host of emotional and psychological problems. Is it any wonder that God so frequently told His people to control their tongues?

What the Bible calls the "sins of the tongue" seem to be especially grievous to God, given the number of verses that warn us not to speak evil about others. God knows that words hurt, and He wants His people to keep a close watch on the words they speak.

Make no mistake about it—you do have to keep a close watch. Sometimes what you say seems innocuous, just another bit of ordinary conversation. You're just stating the facts, right? Jason's been going out with Michelle for two months, and he took Amy to see a movie last night. That's the truth, so it isn't gossip. Or is it? Would you state those same facts if Jason or Amy or Michelle were standing next to you? Case closed.

The truth of the matter is this: Gossip hurts everyone involved. The people you talk about—who most definitely will hear what you said—can be hurt both by what you said (especially if you don't have your facts straight) and simply by the fact that you said it. The people you tell are also affected, because you're coloring their opinion of Jason and Michelle and Amy, and you're luring them into your own wrongdoing by tempting them to repeat the story. Finally, you're hurting yourself, because you are grieving God.

There's one type of situation, though, that requires you to repeat a story—and that's when danger is involved. If you hear that Jeff has threatened to commit suicide, that Alicia's father is abusing her, that somebody in your school is planning to mimic Columbine, tell an adult—a parent, a teacher, the principal, your pastor, the school resource officer, anyone who is in a position to do something about it. You could save someone's life. This is not gossip; this is a moral responsibility.

For the most part, gossip is nowhere near that serious, but it can feel like a punch in the stomach when anyone hears that someone has been talking about him or her. Make sure you're not the one doing the talking—or the listening. Be on the lookout for the seemingly sanitized versions of gossip, the prayer-request variety. You know how that goes: Beth told me that she and Dave have been going at it pretty hot and heavy lately, and she doesn't know how long they'll be able to keep from having sex, and, well, I just don't know how to pray for them, so will you pray with me, that they'll be strong? Please? And that's just the beginning of the prayer chain!

Discipline yourself to walk away from conversations that have degenerated into gossip. Bite your lip and hold your tongue when you are tempted to repeat a story. If you must talk, talk with one hand joined to the other in prayer. And remember Mary. Always hold out the possibility that you're missing one huge, story-changing detail.

I Will

Honor God by keeping a close watch on my words.

<u>yes</u>   <u>no</u>

Remember that prayer requests should be shared only with God.

<u>yes</u>   <u>no</u>

Realize that I seldom have all the facts to determine the truth of a story.

<u>yes</u>   <u>no</u>

Understand that I can guard my friendships by guarding my tongue.

<u>yes</u>   <u>no</u>

Keep in mind that listening to gossip is as wrong as repeating it.

<u>yes</u>   <u>no</u>

Things to Do

☐ Give your tongue back to God! He made it, and He'd like to help you control it.

☐ Ask God to forgive you for the times you've listened to or repeated gossip.

☐ Decide now that you will tell an adult if you ever hear a story that involves a threat or places anyone in danger.

☐ Come up with a script—a practiced response—to use when your friends start to gossip ("Can we talk about something else?").

☐ Write down the names of persons whose words have hurt you. Forgive everyone on your list and make an effort to forget what they said.

Things to Remember

You yourselves are to put off all these: anger, wrath, malice, blasphemy, filthy language out of your mouth.

COLOSSIANS 3:8 NKJV

Where there is no wood, the fire goes out; and where there is no talebearer, strife ceases.

PROVERBS 26:20 NKJV

Let the words of my mouth and the meditation of my heart be acceptable to you, O LORD, my rock and my redeemer.

—PSALM 19:14 NRSV

He who covers a transgression seeks love, but he who repeats a matter separates friends.

PROVERBS 17:9 NKJV

Don't say anything that would hurt another person. Instead, speak only what is good so that you can give help wherever it is needed. That way, what you say will help those who hear you.

EPHESIANS 4:29 GOD'S WORD

A gossip goes around revealing secrets, but those who are trustworthy can keep a confidence.

PROVERBS 11:13 NLT

You shall not go about as a talebearer among your people; nor shall you take a stand against the life of your neighbor: I am the Lord.

LEVITICUS 19:16 NKJV

He who goes about as a talebearer reveals secrets; therefore do not associate with one who flatters with his lips.

PROVERBS 20:19 NKJV

A perverse man sows strife, and a whisperer separates the best of friends.

PROVERBS 16:28 NKJV

Debate your case with your neighbor, and do not disclose the secret to another; lest he who hears it expose your shame, and your reputation be ruined.

PROVERBS 25:9–10 NKJV

The tongue is a small thing, but what enormous damage it can do. A tiny spark can set a great forest on fire.

JAMES 3:5 NLT

If all men knew what others say of them, there would not be four friends in the world.

—BLAISE PASCAL

Whoever gossips to you will gossip about you.

—SPANISH PROVERB

Zero Tolerance

He heals the brokenhearted and binds up their wounds.

—Psalm 147:3 NKJV

Just as Jesus was called to love the seeming unlovable, so, too, are you. Have you ever known people who seem to have zero tolerance for those who aren't exactly like them? If you don't dress or talk or act the way they think you should, you're a total loser in their eyes, and they let you know it. They treat you as if you've just arrived from another planet and you haven't a clue how earthlings are really supposed to live.

You may not be quite that bad, but if you're like most people you could probably do a better job of accepting those who aren't like you. Sometimes the world seems overrun with misfits, outcasts, loners, and assorted other oddballs, and it can be a challenge to accept them and their eccentric behavior.

God made every one of those oddballs. He allowed His Son to die for them, so He obviously thinks they're valuable. That creates a bit of a problem, doesn't it? It's easy to join in when others make fun of those who are different, and it's hard to stand up for what's right when deep down you think some of those people really are kind of weird. No one is asking you to be best buddies with them. But you are asked to accept and respect them like people who are worth dying for.

People can be annoying and rude and mean. They get on your nerves so much that they drive you up a wall and down the other side. Some are dirty and smell funny and have greasy hair. Are you supposed to love and accept them? Yes—every one of them, just the way Jesus accepted the outcasts of His day. You'll know you're on the path to maturity as a believer when you realize that you're learning to love the unlovable.

You can start by looking at people from a more compassionate perspective. Jesus' compassion toward lepers is a great model for you to follow. He saw them as suffering people in need of a savior, while society treated them as if they were hideous, subhuman life-forms. By embracing the very people that the rest of society shunned, Jesus offered the definitive example of the way He expects His followers to show acceptance of other people. There's no place in His kingdom for people with zero tolerance.

I Will

Appreciate the fact that God made each of us to
be unique individuals.   yes   no

Follow Jesus' example of infinite tolerance.   yes   no

Realize that making fun of others is based in
ignorance of Jesus' example.   yes   no

See every human being as worthwhile and
valuable.   yes   no

Be careful of the way I look at those who are
different.   yes   no

Be more compassionate toward outcasts.   yes   no

Things to Do

☐ Read through the Gospels to see how Jesus treated outcasts like
Zaccheus and Mary Magdalene.

☐ Ask God to reveal to you—and help you overcome— any prejudice in
your life.

☐ Pray for the spiritual maturity to follow Jesus' example and to accept
and respect those who are different from you.

☐ Thank God for accepting you and loving you just the way you are.

☐ Confess any judgmental attitude you may have toward people who are
not like you.

Things to Remember

Do not pronounce judgment before the time, before the
Lord comes, who will bring to light the things now hidden
in darkness and will disclose the purposes of the heart.
Then each one will receive commendation from God.

1 CORINTHIANS 4:5 NRSV

Pursue peace with all people, and holiness, without which
no one will see the Lord.

HEBREWS 12:14 NKJV

He has shown you, O man, what is good; and what does
the Lord require of you but to do justly, to love mercy, and
to walk humbly with your God?

MICAH 6:8 NKJV

Jesus said, "Do not judge, so that you may not be judged.
For with the judgment you make you will be judged, and
the measure you give will be the measure you get."

MATTHEW 7:1–2 NRSV

I charge you before God and the Lord Jesus Christ and the
elect angels that you observe these things without
prejudice, doing nothing with partiality.

1 TIMOTHY 5:21 NKJV

Let us treat men and women well; treat them as if they
were real. Perhaps they are.

RALPH WALDO EMERSON

Let God be as original with other people as He is with you.

OSWALD CHAMBERS

Admitting You're Wrong

Be of the same mind toward one another. Do not set your mind on high things, but associate with the humble. Do not be wise in your own opinion.

—Romans 12:16 NKJV

Pride goes before a fall. Yes—God's justice is good! Is there anybody more annoying than a know-it-all? You know the kind—the straight-A student who has an answer for every question in every class, or the girl who has some high and lofty opinion on everything from the clothes you're wearing to the solution for world peace, or the guy who would never in a million years admit that the way he treated his girlfriend was wrong, wrong, wrong.

People like that have a problem much bigger than their annoying behavior—they've got a huge problem with pride. The Bible comes right out and says that God detests pride. Exactly what is—and isn't—sinful pride? And what if you are the one with the problem?

The kind of pride that is sinful is an arrogant, egotistic attitude of superiority. People who are afflicted with it defy anyone who holds any kind of authority over them, or at least they try to. They're always right, never wrong (just ask them) — and they don't exactly spend a lot of time confessing their sin to God. In fact, they are often so blind that they pride themselves on their lack of sin!

That's very different from being proud that you're a Christian or an American or a member of the softball team or a child of your parents. That is not sinful pride, so long as you don't start to think you're better than anyone else because of those things. If you come from a long line of hard-working, sacrificial, God-loving, kind, and gentle people, well, that's something to cheer about.

The dangerous thing about sinful pride is that it can creep up on you in such a sneaky way. Take a scenario like this, for example: Mike, your best friend, knows that you have a problem with lust, because you've talked to him about it. You've never really acted on the temptation, other than to spend way too much time looking at a magazine or two that your uncle had. But all that's over, and you're doing fine — except for one problem. You just got cable on the TV in your bedroom, and you've been doing a lot of late-night channel surfing. Mike sees disaster ahead and tries to warn you.

If you're not careful, your pride will tune out Mike and turn up the volume of self-righteousness in your own head. Who does Mike think he is? I know what I'm doing! It's my life, and he can just shove off. A few months later, after you've logged countless hours watching questionable TV shows, you still refuse to admit you were wrong, even to yourself. Until you confess your pride and pay attention to Mike's warning, you'll be slinking along a surefire path to moral failure.

The Bible tells us that pride goes before a fall; every serious moral and spiritual failure can be traced back to the problem of a prideful ego. If you ever want to know how bad a prideful fall can be, check out the story of the once-powerful King Nebuchadnezzar in Daniel 4. His ego landed him in a pasture, eating grass like an ox, waking up every morning drenched with dew, and sprouting hair like eagles' feathers and nails like birds' claws. He could have learned a lesson from another prideful king, Hezekiah, who repented of his sin and humbled himself before God—and whom God blessed with an abundance of riches. God evidently takes the sin of pride very seriously.

The ability to admit that you are wrong and humble yourself before God is another mark of maturity. By contrast, the inability to acknowledge your mistakes, failures, and sins blocks the flow of God's forgiveness and grace in your life and hinders your spiritual and emotional growth. You need to keep the lines of communication with God wide open, and you can only do that if you are willing to approach Him in all humility and confess your failings to Him.

Being in the wrong is not such a terrible thing; staying in the wrong is. When you are wrong, admit it—then get up, make the wrong things right, and use what you've learned to ward off failure in the future.

I Will

Keep the lines of communication with God open all the time.

yes ___ *no* ___

Humble myself and confess my sins to God.

yes ___ *no* ___

Submit to those in authority over me.

yes ___ *no* ___

Pay attention to those who point out the blind spots in my life.

yes ___ *no* ___

Keep my ego in check.

yes ___ *no* ___

Admit that I really don't know it all.

yes ___ *no* ___

Things to Do

☐ Give God the areas of your life where you might be vulnerable to pride, such as academic or athletic accomplishments. Ask Him to keep you humble.

☐ Read Christian Island: Parables About Pride, Gossip, and Discontentment by Charles Simpson (Ascribe Publishing).

☐ Take a deep breath and go admit to your parents (or a sibling) something that you were wrong about recently.

☐ Ask a trusted friend to point out the blind spots in your life where pride might sneak in.

☐ List some circumstances that can trigger an always-right attitude, so you can be more careful in those situations.

Things to Remember

Listen, for I will speak of excellent things, and from the opening of my lips will come right things; for my mouth will speak truth; wickedness is an abomination to my lips.

PROVERBS 8:6–7 NKJV

The tongue is a fire, a world of iniquity. The tongue is so set among our members that it defiles the whole body, and sets on fire the course of nature; and is set on fire by hell.

JAMES 3:6 NKJV

My words come from my upright heart; my lips utter pure knowledge.

—JOB 33:3 NKJV

The way of a fool is right in his own eyes, but he who heeds counsel is wise.

PROVERBS 12:15 NKJV

First pride, then the crash—the bigger the ego, the harder the fall.

PROVERBS 16:18 THE MESSAGE

Pride leads to disgrace, but with humility comes wisdom.

PROVERBS 11:2 NLT

Jesus said, "I say to you that for every idle word men may speak, they will give account of it in the day of judgment. For by your words you will be justified, and by your words you will be condemned."

MATTHEW 12:36–37 NKJV

Righteous lips are the delight of kings, and they love him who speaks what is right.

PROVERBS 16:13 NKJV

Jesus said, "A good man out of the good treasure of his heart brings forth good; and an evil man out of the evil treasure of his heart brings forth evil. For out of the abundance of the heart his mouth speaks."

LUKE 6:45 NKJV

Haughty eyes, a proud heart, and evil actions are all sin.

PROVERBS 21:4 NLT

Sometimes what seems right is really a road to death.

PROVERBS 16:25 CEV

Never be ashamed to own you have been in the wrong; 'tis but saying you are wiser today than yesterday.

—JONATHAN SWIFT

He that never changed any of his opinions, never corrected any of his mistakes.

—BENJAMIN WHICHCOTE

The Envelope, Please

Commit your works to the LORD, and your thoughts will be
established.

—*Proverbs 16:3* NKJV

God has given you everything you need to succeed in
life, if... Imagine this: You're sitting in the audience with six
thousand of your nearest and dearest—*ahem*—friends. The
camera catches the mingling of fear and hope and
anticipation in what you think is your oh-so-cool
expression. The Academy Award presenter for your
category intones, "The envelope, please!"

If the next words you heard were your name, would
that be your idea of the ultimate achievement? Maybe
you'd prefer an MTV Music Award or a Dove, a Pulitzer or
the Nobel prize, an Olympic gold medal or a World Series
ring. Though the competitions differ, all those awards
signify the same thing—an outstanding achievement
resulting in a very public acknowledgment of success.

If you want to be genuinely successful, though, you
may need to redefine what success is. Some of the most

successful people who have ever lived are those people whose names are known only to God, since their accomplishments were not paraded across a public stage. But they remained faithful to God to the end, and that faithfulness is the standard He uses to measure success. By His standard, spiritual success is not a destination but a journey; you will need to keep maturing as a believer throughout your life. God is far more pleased with a brand-new Christian who is growing in his faith than with a mature believer who is spiritually stagnant.

An unsuccessful, spiritually stagnant Christian is really without excuse. All believers have equal access to the most valuable resource in the world—the wisdom of God. As you draw on His wisdom and apply it to your life, you start to become the person God created you to be, and that's a sure sign of spiritual success. Don't squander the tremendous opportunity you have to do life the right way. You already have everything you need to be a success in life if you have God's Spirit living within you and guiding you along the paths of righteousness.

Is it wrong to desire success in your life's work? No—not if you are motivated by a desire to please God and serve other people. Keep in mind that the most certain path to success is the one God leads you to. Make sure you seek His will for your future. As long as you use your God-given talent, continue to grow in Christ, and trust God with every aspect of your life, your success is all but guaranteed.

I Will

Measure my success by God's standard, not the world's.

    yes   no

Learn to draw on God's wisdom.

    yes   no

Find a balance between working hard and trusting God.

    yes   no

Remember that success is a journey, not a destination.

    yes   no

Consider myself successful as long as I love God and serve others.

    yes   no

Continue to mature as a believer.

    yes   no

Things to Do

- [ ] Ask God what you should be doing right now to help you on your path to success.

- [ ] Define spiritual success in your own words. Make this a personal statement of your goals in Christ.

- [ ] Rate yourself on your current success status. On a scale of 1 to 10, how would you rate your faithfulness to Jesus? Your service to others?

- [ ] Read Success: One Day at a Time by John C. Maxwell.

- [ ] Find a mentor who is willing to help you on whatever field of work you think you might be interested in pursuing.

Things to Remember

Without counsel, plans go awry, but in the multitude of counselors they are established.

PROVERBS 15:22 NKJV

Delight yourself also in the LORD, and He shall give you the desires of your heart.

PSALM 37:4 NKJV

The LORD said to Joshua, "This Book of the Law shall not depart from your mouth, but you shall meditate in it day and night, that you may observe to do according to all that is written in it. For then you will make your way prosperous, and then you will have good success."

JOSHUA 1:8 NKJV

His delight is in the law of the LORD, and in His law he meditates day and night. He shall be like a tree planted by the rivers of water, that brings forth its fruit in its season, whose leaf also shall not wither; and whatever he does shall prosper.

PSALM 1:2–3 NKJV

· ·

It is surprising to observe how much more anybody may become simply being always in His place.

SALINA WATCHMAN

Let us work as if success depended upon ourselves alone; but with heartfelt conviction that we are doing nothing and God everything.

SAINT IGNATIUS OF LOYOLA

Choosing Friends

Do not be deceived: "Evil company corrupts good habits."
—1 Corinthians 15:33 NKJV

Your choice of friends has greater significance than simply the pleasures of the day. Have you ever wondered why you click with some people and not with others? Sure, you probably have the same interests and look at life in pretty much the same way, but there's more to it than that when it comes to those you call your best friends. There's a connection, something you can't really define. You just click.

That connection, even if you don't talk about it much, is probably based on the values you share. You don't have to sit around all day talking about values to know deep down where your friend stands on important things like honesty and loyalty and trust—the glue that holds your relationship together. When you choose your friends based on positive values, you are living out a principle that is repeated throughout the Bible: You need to choose your friends and companions carefully, since your relationships will in large part determine whether you stay the course of faith.

The Old Testament books of 1 and 2 Samuel offer up one

of the most beautiful examples of friendship in the story of David, the shepherd boy who killed Goliath and eventually became king, and Jonathan, David's brother-in-law and a son of King Saul. These two clicked immediately, and their friendship even survived Saul's attempts to kill David, who had become his archrival for the hearts and allegiance of the people. Jonathan saved David's life by helping him escape Saul's wrath; when Philistine soldiers killed Jonathan, David poured out his grief in a passage called the Song of the Bow (2 Samuel 1:19–27). In it, David placed a higher value on his friendship with Jonathan than on his romantic relationships with women.

The kind of friendship David and Jonathan had is possible today, but it requires a love-based commitment that cannot be shaken by changing circumstances. You can start to develop such a friendship by strengthening your relationships with trustworthy and mature friends who encourage you in your walk with the Lord. Those are the kinds of friends who respect your faith, accept you unconditionally, and motivate you to become a better person than you ever thought you could be.

Place a high priority on maintaining your close friendships; be the one who reaches out and encourages and always gives the benefit of the doubt when misunderstandings threaten the relationship. When you go the extra mile for your friends, you prove yourself to be the kind of friend others want to click with.

I Will

Maintain my values even if my friends trash them.   yes   no

Be a positive influence on my friends.   yes   no

Remain committed to my friends despite the circumstances.   yes   no

Be the kind of friend to others that I would like to have for myself.   yes   no

Be the one to reach out and encourage others.   yes   no

Go the extra mile for my friends.   yes   no

Things to Do

☐ Ask God to show you how you can be a better friend.

☐ Choose a close friend to be a prayer and accountability partner.

☐ Read about the deep friendship between Jonathan and David in 1 Samuel 18—20 and see what you can learn about relationships.

☐ Send an encouraging note or e-mail to a friend who's going through a rough time.

☐ Thank one of your friends for things she's done that helped you.

☐ Make a friendship calendar of specific needs and specific times to be there for your friends.

Things to Remember

The righteous should choose his friends carefully, for the way of the wicked leads them astray.

PROVERBS 12:26 NKJV

Blessed is the man who walks not in the counsel of the ungodly, nor stands in the path of sinners, nor sits in the seat of the scornful.

PSALM 1:1 NKJV

As iron sharpens iron, so people can improve each other.

PROVERBS 27:17 NCV

Ointment and perfume delight the heart, and the sweetness of a man's friend gives delight by hearty counsel.

PROVERBS 27:9 NKJV

The slap of a friend can be trusted to help you, but the kisses of an enemy are nothing but lies.

PROVERBS 27:6 NCV

· ·

Many people will walk in and out of your life, but only true friends will leave footprints in your heart.

ELEANOR ROOSEVELT

Friendship is an honest mirror, but it must be allowed to reflect or its power is lost.

MARY HUNT

Weight of the Wait

Do you not know that your body is the temple of the Holy Spirit who is in you, whom you have from God, and you are not your own?

1 Corinthians 6:19 NKJV

By now, you've probably heard the safe-sex message so often that you turn your mind off as soon as you hear the phrase. You've heard all about the potential problems of having unprotected sex, things like disease and unwanted pregnancy. You've also heard all about the various methods people suggest for making sexual activity healthier and safer.

But there's no such thing as safe sex outside of a 100 percent committed marriage relationship. Nothing can keep you safe from all of the consequences of sex before marriage, including a long list of fears. Fear of being found out. Fear of being abandoned by a sexual partner. Fear of genital herpes or AIDS. Fear of pregnancy. Fear that the guilt and shame that weigh you down will never go away.

What's sad is that this is not what God intended when He created this wonderful gift. After all, He's the one who thought all this up, and He wants couples to enjoy it to the fullest. He knows that the way to do that is to hold out for fearless sex, the kind you can only find within the genuinely safe and intimate boundaries of marriage.

Is God asking too much of you? It may seem that way at times, especially if you interpret all the lectures you hear about waiting for marriage as some kind of sadistic punishment to keep you from enjoying physical pleasure. It turns out, though, that God isn't small-minded about sex, people are. God's view of sex is so much bigger and better than the human mind can comprehend. He knows that the true pleasure of the sex act extends beyond the physical into the emotional and spiritual realms, in a way that's downright mysterious.

Some couples try to get around all this by redefining the word *sex*. As long as they don't go all the way, they figure they haven't had sex. They think they can nail their conscience on a technicality. Other couples draw an imaginary line that limits how far they can go, but then they keep moving the line, little by little, until eventually it disappears. Meanwhile, both kinds of couples are playing on a dangerous playground.

Let's get clear on this: Anything that arouses your physical passion in an unhealthy way can be considered too far. For some, this may mean that holding hands and kissing are OK; for others, even that is too much temptation. Regardless, the point should be not to see how far you can go but to learn how to manage your relationship in a way that is totally pleasing to God.

What if you've already blown it? If you're no longer a virgin, all the talk about saving this wonderful gift for your future spouse makes you feel even worse. Well, you have a couple of amazing opportunities before you: You can experience the forgiveness and grace of God on such a deep and awesome level that your life can be changed forever, and you can be there for others who realize too late that they've gone too far.

No matter what your past sexual involvement has been—all or nothing or anything in between—you can start all over today, by settling the issue once and for all. Decide ahead of time how you will handle any and every compromising situation that you may face. Decide that you will not have sex—or engage in any activity that arouses sexual passion—until your wedding night.

This will not be easy. But you can eliminate some of the difficulty by surrounding yourself with like-minded friends who have also made a commitment to sexual purity and to support for each other with prayer and encouragement. You can rest assured that God will help you every step of the way. He always provides an escape route from temptation. He promises that when you focus on your relationship with Him, you can change the way you think and feel about the things that are harmful to you. The more time you spend with Him, the less power today's sexually charged messages will have over you. The more time you spend in His Word, the less confusing those messages will be. And the prospect of having truly safe and fearless sex will make the waiting worthwhile.

I Will

Try to please God in the way I handle my
relationships.

    yes   no

Honor my future marriage partner by waiting to
have sex.

    yes   no

Believe that waiting until marriage is worth the
struggle.

    yes   no

Commit myself to a standard of moral purity.

    yes   no

Guard my mind from impure thoughts about sex.

    yes   no

Focus on my love relationship with God.

    yes   no

Things to Do

☐ Ask God to give you power over sexual temptation.

☐ Memorize helpful scriptures, such as Romans 6:6 and 2 Peter 2:9–10.

☐ Make a commitment to abstinence through the True Love Waits campaign
<http://www.truelovewaits.com/> or a similar, abstinence-based
program.

☐ Find others in your area who have made similar pledges and can help
you live out your commitment.

☐ Write down anything that triggers lustful thoughts (like specific movies
and magazines) and resolve to avoid those things.

Things to Remember

Put to death your members which are on the earth: fornication, uncleanness, passion, evil desire, and covetousness, which is idolatry.

COLOSSIANS 3:5 NKJV

Your old evil desires were nailed to the cross with him; that part of you that loves to sin was crushed and fatally wounded, so that your sin-loving body is no longer under sin's control, no longer needs to be a slave to sin.

ROMANS 6:6 TLB

Put on the Lord Jesus Christ, and make no provision for the flesh, to fulfill its lusts.

—ROMANS 13:14 NKJV

Do you not know that the wicked will not inherit the kingdom of God? Do not be deceived: Neither the sexually immoral nor idolaters nor adulterers nor male prostitutes nor homosexual offenders nor thieves nor the greedy nor drunkards nor slanderers nor swindlers will inherit the kingdom of God.

1 CORINTHIANS 6:9–10 NIV

I have written to you not to keep company with anyone named a brother, who is sexually immoral, or covetous, or an idolater, or a reviler, or a drunkard, or an extortioner—not even to eat with such a person.

1 CORINTHIANS 5:11 NKJV

Don't pour your water in the streets; don't give your love to just any woman.

PROVERBS 5:16 NCV

The way of a guilty man is perverse; but as for the pure, his work is right.

PROVERBS 21:8 NKJV

Flee also youthful lusts; but pursue righteousness, faith, love, peace with those who call on the Lord out of a pure heart.

2 TIMOTHY 2:22 NKJV

The Lord knows how to deliver the godly out of temptations and to reserve the unjust under punishment for the day of judgment.

2 PETER 2:9 NKJV

We have no one to blame but the leering, seducing flare-up of our own lust. Lust gets pregnant, and has a baby: sin! Sin grows up to adulthood, and becomes a real killer.

JAMES 1:14–15 THE MESSAGE

Love can always wait to give; lust can never wait to get.

—AUTHOR UNKNOWN

Kids are dying from causes of sexual activity. You're not going to find a tombstone stating that Frankie died because he was a virgin.

—A. C. GREEN

Why Me?

The LORD said, "It shall come to pass afterward that I will pour out My Spirit on all flesh; your sons and your daughters shall prophesy, your old men shall dream dreams, your young men shall see visions."

Joel 2:28 NKJV

God put you on earth for a specific reason. Do you wonder what that reason is? You may have a fairly good idea of what kind of work you want to do in the future, but that's a whole different thing. When it comes to your purpose in life—the very reason for your existence—you are talking about something much bigger than any career could ever be. Your purpose is the answer to the question, Why was I born?

This is where things get hairy, because no one else can answer that question for you; you have to discover your unique purpose on your own. A great starting point is the Bible, where you can find some general reasons why you were born. You were made to worship God (Psalm 100); to know Him intimately (Philippians 3:10); to share the Good News of why Jesus came to earth (Matthew

28:9); to help people see God because of your good works (Matthew 5:14 and Ephesians 2:10). These and other verses go a long way toward showing you why on earth you are here.

Still, what is that purpose, specific to you, for which you were born? If you've ever seen *It's a Wonderful Life*, you know what purpose is all about, what life in your world would have been like if you had never been born. George Bailey had a few more years behind him than you do, and you probably won't completely understand your purpose for years to come, if ever. You can get an inkling of it, though, by looking at the lives you've touched in the past and the path you're heading toward in the future. If you're involved in church or a youth group, take a good look at the kind of activities or ministries you tend to gravitate toward. Those activities are huge clues to your purpose in the kingdom of God.

The best resource you have for discovering your purpose, of course, is God Himself. He promises that if you seek His will, you will find it. Ask Him to reveal your specific purpose in life. If you keep a journal, be sure to record any impressions you receive after you've prayed. If you've been keeping a journal for a while, go back and read what God has spoken to you in the past. If you still have trouble finding the answers you're seeking, relax. Keep doing what God has you doing. At just the right time, He'll show you His purpose in your life.

I Will

Believe that God created me for a specific
purpose.   ___ yes   ___ no

Relax and trust God to reveal my purpose at the
right time.   ___ yes   ___ no

Remember that my main reason for living is to
love God and be in relationship with Him.   ___ yes   ___ no

Keep doing what God has me doing right now.   ___ yes   ___ no

Place my future in God's hands.   ___ yes   ___ no

Pay attention to the aspects of church life that I
enjoy most.   ___ yes   ___ no

Things to Do

☐ Ask God to reveal how He wants you to serve Him at this point in your life.

☐ Write a letter to God asking Him why you were born and where you're heading. (Be sure to write down any answers He gives you!)

☐ Discover more about your purpose by reading Matthew 6:33, Colossians 3:1–17, Hebrews 10:24–25, Hebrews 13:15, Philippians 2:13, 1 Peter 3:15.

☐ Discover your spiritual gift (1 Corinthians 12) using a test provided by your church or youth group, or download one found online at ⟨http://www.abba.ca/localfiles.htm⟩.

☐ Identify what you enjoy most at church or youth group. Find common threads to help you discover your purpose.

Things to Remember

Paul wrote: One thing I do, forgetting those things which are behind and reaching forward to those things which are ahead, I press toward the goal for the prize of the upward call of God in Christ Jesus.

PHILIPPIANS 3:13–14 NKJV

In Him also we have obtained an inheritance, being predestined according to the purpose of Him who works all things according to the counsel of His will, that we who first trusted in Christ should be to the praise of His glory.

EPHESIANS 1:11–12 NKJV

God is at work within you, helping you want to obey him, and then helping you do what he wants.

PHILIPPIANS 2:13 TLB

God planned for us to do good things and to live as he has always wanted us to live. That's why he sent Christ to make us what we are.

EPHESIANS 2:10 CEV

Jesus said, "Let your light so shine before men, that they may see your good works and glorify your Father in heaven."

MATTHEW 5:16 NKJV

· ·

The only glory which Jesus ever sought for himself or offered to his disciples was to be caught up into God's redemptive purpose.

GEORGE CAIRD

Must-Haves

Jesus said, "Seek first the kingdom of God and His righteousness, and all these things shall be added to you."
—Matthew 6:33 NKJV

Waiting and trusting God will put any must-haves in true perspective. But do you have a baby brother or sister? If so, you know what a racket babies make when they want something. They want milk, and they want it now! Giving them what they're demanding now is called instant gratification. They get it almost as soon as they want it. That desire for instant gratification doesn't end when babies graduate from the cradle.

Just like babies, people want to have everything they desire now. You want high-speed Internet access because you need information (OK, downloaded music) now. You have to have a microwave oven because you want your burrito now. You can't wait for spring break or Christmas or the day you get your license or your eighteenth birthday. And that movie you've been dying to see on DVD—well, you can order it online a month before it's released. So what happens when you get it? The high lasts, oh, maybe a day or two. Then, you are on to wanting something else. You're not alone in all this, of course. The desire for instant gratification is quite human.

You don't scream and cry like a baby, but perhaps your attitude may be sometimes just as bad as a baby's when you have to wait for something. The ability to calmly wait for the thing you want so much—called delayed or deferred gratification—is one of the most distinctive indications of a person's maturity. Mature kids are those who have learned to wait, whether it's for their first car or their turn in the spotlight or until marriage to have sex.

The demand for instant gratification also can short-circuit your faith. God has a plan for your life, and He will unfold it as you trust Him. But you also have to trust His timing, and that can mean a whole lot of waiting as He works on bringing you to a place of maturity where He can fulfill His plan.

Denying yourself pleasure or privileges or stuff isn't easy, especially when your friends seem to have it all. But once you've sorted out your genuine needs from the mass of things you feel you must have, you begin to realize that your must-haves aren't all that satisfying. The next time you get that red-hot desire to acquire, call a time-out on yourself. All you may really need is a cooldown period of waiting and trusting God.

I Will

Trust God to provide everything I need.
yes ___ *no* ___

Learn to cool down and wait on God when I feel I
have to have a certain thing.
yes ___ *no* ___

Acknowledge my need to accept deferred
gratification.
yes ___ *no* ___

Rely on God's timing rather than my own.
yes ___ *no* ___

Find contentment in what I already have.
yes ___ *no* ___

Bring my impatience under control.
yes ___ *no* ___

Things to Do

☐ Ask God to help you resist the influence of the now culture in which
you live.

☐ Make a list of your genuine needs and hand the list over to God.

☐ Take an inventory of what you already have—say, all your CDs or
videos. Do you really need more?

☐ Make a list of the things you think you want, cut it in half, then half
again to reduce the list to those things you really want.

☐ Establish a specific waiting period, such as a week or a month, before
you buy anything that is not essential.

☐ Give the clothes you no longer want or wear to a worthwhile charity.

Things to Remember

Paul wrote: Not that I speak in regard to need, for I have learned in whatever state I am, to be content.

PHILIPPIANS 4:11 NKJV

Serving God does make us very rich, if we are satisfied with what we have.

1 TIMOTHY 6:6 NCV

Jesus said, "Blessed are those who hunger and thirst for righteousness, for they shall be filled."

MATTHEW 5:6 NKJV

The LORD said, "Why do you spend money for what is not bread, and your wages for what does not satisfy? Listen carefully to Me, and eat what is good, and let your soul delight itself in abundance."

ISAIAH 55:2 NKJV

Command those who are rich in this present age not to be haughty, nor to trust in uncertain riches but in the living God, who gives us richly all things to enjoy.

1 TIMOTHY 6:17 NKJV

. . . .

Unbridled gratification produces unbridled desire.

TRADITIONAL PROVERB

One sign of maturity is delayed gratification.

PEGGY CAHN

Upside-Down World

God is not the author of confusion but of peace, as in all the churches of the saints.

1 Corinthians 14:33 NKJV

Biblical truth can always be counted on to make sense out of nonsense. But you might as well come right out and admit it: There are days when you feel as if you're the only sane person left on Earth. Everything seems to have gone haywire; what was right is now wrong, and what was wrong is now right, and nobody appears to have his act together. The world around you is turning upside down, just as you are trying to navigate your way to adulthood. Great timing, right?

The good news is that you'll most likely handle the craziness of life better than anyone expects you to, because that may be all you've ever known. Since the day you were born, you've no doubt been bombarded with sounds and images, advertisements and commercials, contradictions and paradoxes—and a moral code that's nearly indecipherable. But no matter how accustomed you are to chaos, you still need a rock-solid framework for your life, one that won't collapse with the cultural shifts you're going to face. That's why you have to make it a point to understand the Bible, because that's the one guide for living that has withstood the test of time, as well as every other test it's been put through.

It is equally important to clear up any confusion you may have about God. For starters, ditch the image of God as a supernatural Santa. He doesn't hand out gifts after checking His list twice to see who's been naughty or nice. He loves the most hardened criminal on death row just as much as He loves Billy Graham, and every bit of love that He has given to Billy Graham he has given to that inmate, too. The difference between the hardened criminal and Billy Graham lies not in God's love for them but in each person's openness to God and the gifts He gives. So forget Santa.

God is also not a harsh taskmaster. Kids who have had difficult fathers often carry the concept of a strict disciplinarian over to their image of God. But God is a merciful, gracious Father who doesn't exact a penalty for every wrong thing you've ever done or bad thought you've ever had.

Make no mistake about it, though: God is no weakling. He's the all-powerful, all-knowing, ever-present Creator of the universe. And even so He's available to you. He wants to help you navigate your way through life by transforming your bewilderment into wisdom and understanding. That's why He gave us the Bible and His Spirit.

You have a responsibility in all this, and that is to make a connection between what you read in His Word and how you live your life. Without that connection, you'll find it difficult, if not impossible, to sort out the confusion. Understanding this concept—that your belief in the truth and authenticity of the Bible must have an impact on your everyday life—is critical to your spiritual well-being.

If you're not convinced about this, look at a facet of American life that's out of whack, like the diminished value placed on an individual life by the acceptance of promiscuous behavior—which degrades girls and guys—or the prevalence of abortion among unwed teenage girls. Can you see the disconnect between those practices and the way the Bible affirms the value of every single person? Confusion swirls around those issues because people do not let biblical truth influence their lives.

Take another example. The Bible gives clear guidelines for parents on how they should love, care for, and provide for their children. But today, even young children are left alone to fend for themselves, because some parents have done a role reversal on them. These "adults" are off acting like kids, forcing their children to take care of themselves. There's little connection in their lives between biblical principles and daily life.

Unless you allow biblical truth to saturate your mind and your spirit and your behavior, you'll also find it difficult to make those connections. Simply calling yourself a Christian isn't enough; a mere label won't help you make sense out of life. Commit yourself to making sure that the connection between the Bible and your life is intact, and you can trade in your confusion for a life that's right side up.

I Will

Make sure I have a proper understanding of who God is.

yes _____ no _____

Take the Bible seriously and allow its truth to affect my everyday life.

yes _____ no _____

Learn to see the connection between moral confusion and lack of biblical understanding.

yes _____ no _____

Rely on the Bible and God's Spirit to help me navigate my way through a confusing world.

yes _____ no _____

Learn to question the mixed messages I'm bombarded with each day.

yes _____ no _____

Things to Do

☐ Ask God to help you understand those things that you find particularly confusing about your life.

☐ Honestly assess how much you allow the Bible to influence the way you live. Make a written commitment to improve in this area.

☐ Select one political or moral issue and compare the pro and con arguments you hear against what the Bible has to say.

☐ Write down the impressions you have of God. Make it a priority to correct the way you see Him if it conflicts with the way God is revealed in the Bible.

☐ Compare the lyrics of a popular song with the biblical model of right and wrong to gain a fuller understanding of the way the "disconnect" influences our culture.

Things to Remember

Do not be conformed to this world, but be transformed by the renewing of your mind, that you may prove what is that good and acceptable and perfect will of God.

ROMANS 12:2 NKJV

Let all things be done decently and in order.

1 CORINTHIANS 14:40 NKJV

Those of steadfast mind you keep in peace—in peace because they trust in you.

—ISAIAH 26:3 NRSV

Do not let your good be spoken of as evil; for the kingdom of God is not eating and drinking, but righteousness and peace and joy in the Holy Spirit.

ROMANS 14:16–17 NKJV

A meal of bread and water in contented peace is better than a banquet spiced with quarrels.

PROVERBS 17:1 THE MESSAGE

The steps of the godly are directed by the
LORD. He delights in every detail of their
lives.

PSALM 37:23 NLT

Jesus said, "The Helper, the Holy Spirit,
whom the Father will send in My name, He
will teach you all things, and bring to your
remembrance all things that I said to you.
Peace I leave with you, My peace I give to
you; not as the world gives do I give to you.
Let not your heart be troubled, neither let it
be afraid."

JOHN 14:26–27 NKJV

Where envy and self-seeking exist, confusion
and every evil thing are there.

JAMES 3:16 NKJV

That there should be no schism in the body,
but that the members should have the same
care for one another.

1 CORINTHIANS 12:25 NKJV

Even as I have seen, those who plow
iniquity and sow trouble reap the same.

JOB 4:8 NKJV

In thee, O LORD, do I put my trust: let me
never be put to confusion.

PSALM 71:1 KJV

Good order is
the foundation
of all good
things.

—EDMUND BURKE

The devil is the
author of
confusion.

—ROBERT BURTON

The Ex Files

We are not crushed and broken. We are perplexed, but we don't give up and quit.

—2 Corinthians 4:8 NLT

There's no getting around it: Breaking up is hard to do. Having your heart broken for the first time—when this whole love thing is still so fresh and new—is especially painful. What's worse, everyone knows. You feel like dying, and it seems the whole world is watching.

At times like that, you'd probably like to buy a heart-repair kit. After a few days, you'd be all better, with a fully mended heart and the vague feeling that something kind of bad happened awhile back. The reality is, however, that you were born with a heart that can't be repaired that easily.

What can you do when your heart is broken? Well, you could give up or just give it time. Or you could live a lie, treating your ex as if your relationship never mattered. But that heart you were born with still has a need for love. The hurt and pain may have rearranged things a bit, but your heart is intact.

You may not believe God can touch you, but He can. When you're suffering a deep emotional pain, He takes your heart and smoothes away the bumps and bruises. You have to first give it to Him, trusting that His hands can prepare your heart to love again. When you do love again, you will know more about love than you ever thought possible.

In the meantime, take special care of yourself. Get the rest you need; stay away from caffeine or anything else that interferes with sleep or contributes to depression. Eliminate junk food, which can cause your blood sugar—and emotions—to plummet. Several times a week, go for a walk. You'll feel better all around.

Be careful what—and who—you listen to. You may need to steer clear of the music you normally listen to and find something that will lift your spirits. Although your friends may have good intentions, they can feed your sadness by putting down your ex or passing along news you don't want to hear. It's good to discuss your feelings with a trusted friend, but choose that friend wisely. Make sure you bare your soul to an encouraging friend who can keep a confidence.

Will you ever forget the first time your heart was broken? No. But the pain will diminish as you allow God to start healing your broken heart.

I Will

Give my heart to God to repair.

yes   *no*

Trust God with my heart in the future.

yes   *no*

Realize that recovering from a breakup
will take time.

yes   *no*

Believe that things will get better.

yes   *no*

Be careful to guard my heart.

yes   *no*

Be careful with other people's hearts.

yes   *no*

Treat anyone I've dated with respect.

yes   *no*

Things to Do

☐ Give your heart to God for safekeeping.

☐ Ask God for wisdom before you give your heart away.

☐ Pray that you'll see God's love for you today.

☐ List qualities (like faithfulness) you require in a person before you
agree to go out with him or her. Resolve not to compromise on those
qualities.

☐ Read Justin Lookadoo's Dateable.

☐ Thank God for His concern for the brokenhearted.

☐ Decide now to always treat an ex with respect.

Things to Remember

David wrote: My flesh and my heart fail; but God is the strength of my heart and my portion forever.

PSALM 73:26 NKJV

May the God of hope fill you with all joy and peace in believing, that you may abound in hope by the power of the Holy Spirit.

ROMANS 15:13 NKJV

The LORD is near to those who have a broken heart, and saves such as have a contrite spirit.

PSALM 34:18 NKJV

This is my comfort in my misery: Your promise gave me a new life.

PSALM 119:50 GOD'S WORD

The Lord said, "Then shall the virgin rejoice in the dance, and the young men, and the old, together; for I will turn their mourning to joy, will comfort them, and make them rejoice rather than sorrow."

JEREMIAH 31:13 NKJV

Love is like a violin. The music may stop now and then, but the strings remain forever.

JUNE MASTERS BACHER

Do your utmost to guard your heart, for out of it comes life.

WALTER HILTON

What Do They Know, Anyway?

"Honor your father and mother," which is the first commandment with promise: "that it may be well with you and you may live long on the earth."

Ephesians 6:2–3 NKJV

Wouldn't it be great if you knew someone who could help you sort out everything you're going through right now, someone who could tell you what to expect in the years to come and steer you in the right direction? God always has the wisdom you seek. Sometimes, though, you could use a flesh-and-blood person as a sounding board for the thoughts and ideas and questions that often swirl through your mind.

Well, you do have such a person, or maybe even two—your mother or father or both. Open communication is the key to tapping in to their years of experience and drawing out the wisdom they've acquired. Keeping the lines of communication open is essential to keep things from falling apart at home. And keeping the lines of communication open and clear—without any static on either side—may depend on you more than you realize.

Take a scenario like this: You want to go to college, but you're not sure what you want to do with your life. You'd like to take off a year after high school, work full-time, save some money, and then go to college after you've sorted out your goals. You tell your parents what you're thinking—and your father hits the ceiling. He won't hear of such a plan. You're going to college, and that's that! Your mother has her own concerns, though she reacts by looking away and fighting back the tears. She quietly leaves the room as your father goes on and on about how you'll never get anywhere in life without a college degree. You get mad, because you think he obviously wasn't listening to you in the first place, and you stalk off to your room. The conversation is over. Nothing is settled.

From your perspective, your parents are being downright unreasonable. Well, maybe they didn't handle the situation the way you wish they had, but you have no way of knowing what they were thinking or why they reacted the way they did. You realize that your father never graduated from college—but maybe what you don't know is that he dropped out after two years, figuring he could bum around the country for a while and get his head together. You also realize that your mother never went to college—but maybe what you don't know is that she had always planned to; she just wanted to work for a year after high school and enroll in college later. But then she met your father, and, well, that was the end of college for both of them.

Can you see the dynamics in this scenario from a

different perspective now? Your parents, or rather your hypothetical parents, are trying to spare you the disappointment they experienced because of the questionable choices they made. They want the best for you, and they don't want you repeating their mistakes. And this is exactly why you may need to take the initiative with them. They may not want to think about their failures, let alone share them with you.

So how do you draw on their wisdom? First, make sure your attitude toward them is grounded in respect, which is what honoring your parents is all about. Unless you start from a foundation of respect—treating them with courtesy, always speaking well of them, following their godly example—then your efforts at communication will fall on deaf ears (theirs!). Second, seek God's guidance on the best way, and the best time, to approach them. God is the only one who can see the heart of each person involved, and He can offer insight and practical direction that no one else can.

Third, trust God with the outcome. Maybe your efforts at honest communication will fail. It's even possible that your parents may try to steer you away from what you believe is God's will for your life. Remember this—everyone, including your parents, will eventually disappoint you in some way, just as you will disappoint them. But God never disappoints. When you keep your focus on the primary relationship in your life—the one you have with the Lord—you have the confidence of knowing that the wisdom you seek is as close as He is.

I Will

Honor my parents by showing them respect.   yes ___ no ___

Turn to my parents for wisdom and guidance.   yes ___ no ___

Learn to genuinely listen to what my parents are
trying to tell me.   yes ___ no ___

Realize that my parents are going through
changes too.   yes ___ no ___

Initiate the process of resolving conflicts with my
parents.   yes ___ no ___

Express my appreciation to my parents for what
they've done for me.   yes ___ no ___

Things to Do

☐ Ask God to show you how you can keep communication open with your
parents.

☐ Make a written commitment to treat your parents with the same courtesy
and respect you give to other adults.

☐ List the things that cause problems with your parents (money, curfew,
grades). Next to each item, list what you can do to about those
problems.

☐ Show appropriate physical affection—hug your mother, place your hand
on your father's shoulder.

☐ List all the things your parents provide for you. Be as specific as
possible. Find a way to thank them.

Things to Remember

Hear, my son, and receive my sayings, and the years of your life will be many.

PROVERBS 4:10 NKJV

Endure trials for the sake of discipline. God is treating you as children; for what child is there whom a parent does not discipline?

HEBREWS 12:7 NRSV

Every one of you shall revere his mother and his father, and keep My Sabbaths: I am the Lord your God.

—LEVITICUS 19:3 NKJV

A father of the fatherless, a defender of widows, is God in His holy habitation.

PSALM 68:5 NKJV

Whoever curses his father or his mother, his lamp will be put out in deep darkness.

PROVERBS 20:20 NKJV

Solomon wrote: Hear me now, my children, and do not depart from the words of my mouth.

PROVERBS 5:7 NKJV

Everyone must submit himself to the governing authorities, for there is no authority except that which God has established. The authorities that exist have been established by God.

ROMANS 13:1 NIV

A son honors his father, and a servant his master. If then I am the Father, where is My honor? And if I am a Master, where is My reverence? says the LORD of hosts to you priests who despise My name. Yet you say, "In what way have we despised Your name?"

MALACHI 1:6 NKJV

Even if my father and mother abandon me, the LORD will take care of me.

PSALM 27:10 GOD'S WORD

Keep your father's command, and do not forsake the law of your mother.

PROVERBS 6:20–21 NKJV

Love begins at home, and it is not how much we do but how much love we put in that action.

—MOTHER TERESA

Parents—they're strict on you when you're little, and you don't understand why. But as you get older, you understand and you appreciate it.

—GRANT HILL

Here on Earth

Jesus said, *"Most assuredly, I say to you, he who believes in Me, the works that I do he will do also; and greater works than these he will do, because I go to My Father."*
—John 14:12 NKJV

"It's a miracle!" Maybe you've heard someone say that about acing a math test or sneaking out of the house without getting caught. Casually using the word *miracle* waters down its primary meaning—an extraordinary event brought on by divine intervention. Then again, maybe the Divine did intervene in those situations, and someone needs to thank Him! Miracles abound in the commonplace.

In another way, the casual use of the word can serve as a reminder of God's involvement in daily things like the sun rising every twenty-four hours and gravity keeping you firmly planted on solid ground. You wake up every morning and don't give your existence a second thought, though it's pretty amazing that your vital organs didn't shut down during the night for no reason, the way a cranky computer might.

Think about your life. You've come a long way since you were a baby. You've even come a long way since last year. Maybe your life today is radically different than what you expected it to be; you used to be awkward, but now you're an accomplished athlete. Or you used to be shy, but now you're a natural at acting. You may take those things for granted, but your progress is nothing short of miraculous. Isn't it possible that God is responsible for that? He has intervened in your life in ways you may never know: prompting you to try something new; helping you remember a critical fact during a test; even keeping the car from starting just long enough to prevent you from being involved in a crash.

When you begin to see the miraculous in the commonplace, you take on a whole new appreciation for God's love. That doesn't mean that you'll suddenly see His activity in every little thing you do, but it does mean that once in a while you'll be more likely to recognize the way He's involved in your life and in everyday, ordinary things. He's involved not because He has to be but because He wants to be.

Many people go through the motions of daily living without stopping to think about how incredible life is. They get jaded quickly and start asking, Is this all there is? But those who have learned to acknowledge the miraculous in everyday life discover that they can never again think of life as routine. Instead, they find countless reasons to rejoice and think, Look at all there is!

I Will

Learn to recognize the way God shows His love in
my daily life.

yes   *no*

Give God the credit for the good things that have
happened to me.

yes   *no*

Appreciate God's activity in my life.

yes   *no*

Look for reasons to rejoice in the life God has
given me.

yes   *no*

Stop taking my life for granted.

yes   *no*

Practice seeing routine things from a spiritual
perspective.

yes   *no*

Things to Do

☐ Read Matthew 6:25–34 for a clear picture of just how interested God is
in the details of your everyday life.

☐ Write down the signs of God you see in your life. Start with a recent
situation in which He intervened.

☐ Watch the news tonight and look for indications of God's behind-the-
scenes activity.

☐ Thank God specifically for the vast number of things that work correctly
each day.

☐ List all the things that must happen before you can even get out of bed
(you wake up, your eyelids open—this could be a long list!).

Things to Remember

Come and see the works of God; He is awesome in His doing toward the sons of men.

PSALM 66:5 NKJV

Look to the LORD and his strength; seek his face always. Remember the wonders he has done, his miracles, and the judgments he pronounced.

1 CHRONICLES 16:11–12 NIV

David wrote: I will remember the works of the LORD, surely I will remember your wonders of old.

PSALM 77:11 NKJV

He does great works too marvelous to understand. He performs miracles without number.

JOB 5:9 NLT

You are the God who does wonders; You have declared Your strength among the peoples.

PSALM 77:14 NKJV

• •

The invariable mark of wisdom is to see the miraculous in the common.

RALPH WALDO EMERSON

To me every hour of the light and the dark is a miracle, Every cubic inch of space is a miracle.

WALT WHITMAN

High Fidelity

A man who has friends must himself be friendly, but there is a friend who sticks closer than a brother.

—Proverbs 18:24 NKJV

True loyalty, true fidelity, lasts, no matter what. Anyone who's into music knows about high fidelity. A sound system touted as high fidelity is one that promises to reproduce a sound that is faithful to that of the original performance; every detail of the recording is precisely replicated—or so the salesclerk says.

Such a degree of fidelity, or faithfulness, is difficult to achieve, in life as well as in a sound system. You'd probably love to be a precise reproduction of Jesus Christ. Even if you can't be a faithful reproduction, you can be a faithful follower by the way you live. That doesn't mean you have to go around spouting scripture verses all day, but it does mean that your behavior, activities, and lifestyle should be faithful to the principles found in the Bible—the original and only mistake-free guide for living.

The biblical principle for loyalty stems from God's

commandment to love Him and to love others as He loves you. God doesn't want you to be faithful to Him alone; He wants you to be loyal to your family, your friends, and anyone in authority over you. That kind of loyalty is lived out in the nitty-gritty details of life. What if public scandal hits your family? What if your brother—the one people always compare you to—comes home one night totally plastered? Or your sister—the one who always gets her way—is caught shoplifting? Will you stand by them, or will your shame or anger stand in the way? By turning to God when people have betrayed or disappointed you, you can find the power to continue to love them when they need you most.

In some situations, you may feel completely helpless. You don't know what to say, so you back off rather than risk saying the wrong thing. You may not need to say or do a thing, except to listen when someone is ready to talk. That example of faithfulness is one your friend or relative will remember for a long time to come. As long as you stay sensitive to the leading of God's Spirit, you can't go wrong.

Loyalty perseveres, no matter how much a relationship is tested, because loyalty is based on unwavering commitment. You can count on your relationships being tested, especially your relationship with God. The commitment you make today will help build a strong foundation of faithfulness for future times of testing.

I Will

Discover God's principles for living and follow them.

yes _____ _no_ _____

Prove my faithfulness to God by the way I live.

yes _____ _no_ _____

Keep the commitments I've made.

yes _____ _no_ _____

Prepare myself for those times when my relationships will be tested.

yes _____ _no_ _____

Be there when a friend or relative needs to know they're not alone.

yes _____ _no_ _____

Forget my own embarrassment and stand by my family.

yes _____ _no_ _____

Things to Do

- [ ] Memorize at least one portion of Scripture that tells of the faithfulness of God, such as Psalm 36.

- [ ] Ask God to help you be faithful in the little things so you'll be prepared to handle the big things.

- [ ] Make a list of specific ways you can show your loyalty to God, to your friends, and to your family.

- [ ] Make a private (or public) pledge to remain faithful to God. Write it down, date it, and sign it.

- [ ] Listen to some CDs that have loyalty as a theme and think about how the lyrics apply to your life (some suggestions: The Faithful by Steve Green, Faithful Heart by Alicia, Faithful by Pam Thum).

Things to Remember

Not so with My servant Moses; he is faithful in all My house. I speak with him face to face.

NUMBERS 12:7 NKJV

Therefore know that the LORD your God, He is God, the faithful God who keeps covenant and mercy for a thousand generations with those who love Him and keep His commandments.

DEUTERONOMY 7:9 NKJV

Beloved, you are acting faithfully in whatever you accomplish for the brethren, and especially when they are strangers.

3 JOHN 1:5 NASB

Jesus said, "He who is faithful in what is least is faithful also in much; and he who is unjust in what is least is unjust also in much."

LUKE 16:10 NKJV

Oh, love the LORD, all you His saints! For the LORD preserves the faithful, and fully repays the proud person.

PSALM 31:23 NKJV

· ·

It is, however, only by fidelity in little things that a true and constant love of God can be distinguished from a passing fervor of spirit.

FRANÇOIS FÉNELON

It is better to be faithful than famous.

THEODORE ROOSEVELT

Time to Chill

He who is slow to anger is better than the mighty, and he who rules his spirit than he who takes a city.

—Proverbs 16:32 NKJV

On nearly any day that you can think of, things go right more often than they go wrong. But by third period, it was already a horrible day. You got a bad grade on the paper you turned in last week. Then your math teacher had the nerve to give a pop quiz. So you went to lunch and found some new kid sitting where you always sit. To top it off, you checked the audition results, and someone who can't even sing got the part you wanted!

That sure passes the test for a rotten day. You felt totally within your rights when you wanted to slam the door, throw your books across the room, and cuss when you finally got home. No one was going to take away your right to freak out.

But wait a minute—take a closer look at your day. Deep down, you know you deserved the grade you got on the paper since you didn't start it until the night before it was due. You may have done well on the math quiz, for all you know. At lunch, your friends made room for you, and as for the play—well, you got a pretty good part anyway.

How does your reaction stack up against those things that went wrong? Did you go a little over the top? Chances are, taking time to chill—calming yourself down before you did something really dumb—along about lunchtime would have turned your day around. Instead, you left a trail of bad impressions wherever you went (like with the new kid).

Overreacting draws attention to the crummy things that happen to us, but it doesn't really satisfy us. Have you ever felt better after you made a scene in public? You probably felt like a complete fool, even while you were doing it. But once you got started, you figured you'd feel more foolish if you stopped in the middle of your big scene.

When you blow things out of proportion, you lose any hope of finding joy, peace, or contentment, and you lose the opportunity to learn from your mistakes. While you're ranting and raving, you can't even hear your own conscience telling you to stop.

For the next few days, decide that no matter what happens, you are not going to freak out. Then look around—you probably won't have to look far—for kids who are overreacting to the everyday frustrations of life. What are you thinking as you watch them? Boy, what an idiot. Look at her, she's just trying to get attention. He ought to chill. It doesn't look good on other people, does it? It doesn't look so good on you, either.

Overreacting can become a habit, and what starts out as a seemingly harmless display of melodrama can have serious consequences. People can get hurt; things can get broken; friends can be lost. And you might face an unpleasant or even harsh punishment if that melodrama turned out to be especially destructive.

Before you make a scene is the perfect time to cool off and get spiritual. God has given you a conscience for a good reason—He wants you to use it! When you sense you're about to go over the edge, take the escape route God has placed before you. Follow your conscience this time; back away from the edge and breathe a sigh of relief that you didn't plunge headlong into an embarrassing display of irrational behavior. Oh, and you might want to thank God for the timely reminder.

It's healthy to vent your feelings—but only in an appropriate way, by writing in a journal or by telling God just how you feel. The next time you feel the need to air your emotions in public, stop and think about the consequences. Calm yourself down and make a conscious decision to let it all out once you get alone. By then, of course, you probably won't need to, but at least you wouldn't have denied yourself the right to freak out.

When you really think about it, on most days the things that go right far outnumber the things that go wrong. When you put the emphasis on the few things that are frustrating, you set yourself up for trouble. That's when you know it's time to follow your own advice: Take time to chill.

I Will

Trust God to help me find appropriate ways to
handle frustration. Calm myself down more often.   yes _____   no _____

Work on my need for greater self-control.   yes _____   no _____

Listen to my conscience.   yes _____   no _____

Pay attention to the things that go right.   yes _____   no _____

Stop making a big deal out of nothing.   yes _____   no _____

Stop drawing the wrong kind of attention to
myself.   yes _____   no _____

Things to Do

☐ Ask God to forgive you for overreacting.

☐ List all the things that went right today and thank God for everything on
the list.

☐ List everything that went wrong today and figure out what you could
learn from those things.

☐ Resolve to walk away from a situation when you feel yourself start to
lose it.

☐ Decide that you will take a time-out and count to ten the next time
things go wrong.

Things to Remember

Do not be overcome by evil, but overcome evil with good.

ROMANS 12:21 NKJV

Fools start fights everywhere while wise men try to keep peace.

PROVERBS 29:8 TLB

Be angry, and do not sin. Meditate within your heart on your bed.

—PSALM 4:4 NKJV

You must stay calm and be willing to suffer. You must work hard to tell the good news and to do your job well.

2 TIMOTHY 4:5 CEV

David wrote: O God, my heart is steadfast; I will sing and give praise, even with my glory.

PSALM 108:1 NKJV

Thus says the LORD God, the Holy One of Israel: "In returning and rest you shall be saved; in quietness and in confidence shall be your strength."

ISAIAH 30:15 NKJV

A wise man controls his temper. He knows that anger causes mistakes.

PROVERBS 14:29 TLB

In God (I will praise His word), in God I have put my trust; I will not fear. What can flesh do to me?

PSALM 56:4 NKJV

We are in danger of being called in question for today's uproar, there being no reason which we may give to account for this disorderly gathering.

ACTS 19:40 NKJV

A wrathful man stirs up strife, but he who is slow to anger allays contention.

PROVERBS 15:18 NKJV

Cease from anger, and forsake wrath; do not fret—it only causes harm.

PSALM 37:8 NKJV

If you are patient in one moment of anger, you will avoid one hundred days of sorrow.

—CHINESE PROVERB

Borrow trouble for yourself, if that's your nature, but don't lend it to your neighbors.

—RUDYARD KIPLING

Quote, Unquote

Shun profane and idle babbles, for they will increase to more ungodliness.

—2 Timothy 2:16 NKJV

Rumors often are untrue, yet they can circulate halfway around the world before anyone has a chance to verify the facts. On an unimaginably huge scale, the Internet gives rumors the potential to span the globe at lightning speed. Remember the one that announced Whitney Houston's death when she was a no-show at a concert in 2001? Her fans sobbed as her agent repeatedly denied the rumor—one that was proven false at her next live appearance. And what about urban legends? They're little more than rumors that have taken on a life of their own.

Rumors are also nothing new, and no one is immune to being their victim. Jesus Himself was the victim of rumors about His behavior and teachings. In one incident, word spread among His followers that He had said the disciple John would never die. It's even possible that another disciple, Peter, started the rumor, either because he misunderstood a comment Jesus made or because others created their own version of his accurate account.

A rumor is circulated as truth, but often there is no basis in fact. Repeating a rumor can have devastating consequences in another person's life. Geoff is one guy who could tell you just how harmful a rumor can be.

Shortly after Geoff moved to a new town, some guys spread the story that his twin brother had hanged himself when he was six years old. Immediately, Geoff was branded as creepy; after all, what must he be like if his twin brother did that? The truth was that Geoff was a perfectly normal teenager who never had a twin brother. But suddenly, in the midst of all the difficulties that come with starting over in a new school, he had to put up with a bunch of freshmen staring at him as if he were a mental case. By the time Geoff got wind of the rumor and tried to convince everybody that it wasn't true, it was too late—lots of people didn't believe him, and the "creepy" label became impossible to shake.

Any time you spread a rumor—even a seemingly harmless one—you're asking for trouble. A rumor can backfire on you in ways you can't imagine, possibly costing you your friends, your reputation, and your witness as a Christian. It's not worth it, especially since this is one of the easiest sins to avoid. If you never start a rumor, never repeat one, and never pay attention to one, you're home free.

I Will

Ask God to set a guard over my mouth.   yes _____ no _____

Realize that all rumors are potentially harmful.   yes _____ no _____

Learn to question the validity of the stories I hear.   yes _____ no _____

Be sensitive to the way others can be hurt by
rumors.   yes _____ no _____

Avoid judging people by the stories I hear about
them.   yes _____ no _____

Remember that I also hurt myself when I repeat a
story.   yes _____ no _____

Things to Do

☐ Make a written commitment to yourself and to God that you will not be
involved in spreading untrue stories.

☐ Ask God to forgive you for times that you may have helped spread
false stories.

☐ Forgive someone who has spread a rumor about you; then forget
about it.

☐ Decide now that you will quietly walk away whenever your friends start
talking about the latest rumor.

☐ Go out of your way to be kind to someone that you've recently heard
an ugly story about.

Things to Remember

The crooked heart will not prosper; the twisted tongue tumbles into trouble.

PROVERBS 17:20 NLT

Set a guard, O LORD, over my mouth; keep watch over the door of my lips.

PSALM 141:3 NKJV

The rumor spread among the brotherhood that that disciple wouldn't die! But that isn't what Jesus said at all! He only said, "If I want him to live until I come, what is that to you?"

JOHN 21:23 TLB

Whoever guards his mouth and tongue keeps his soul from troubles.

PROVERBS 21:23 NKJV

Don't lose courage; rumors will spread through the land, but don't be afraid. One rumor comes this year, and another comes the next year. There will be rumors of terrible fighting in the country, of rulers fighting against rulers.

JEREMIAH 51:46 NCV

• •

Rumor grows as it goes.

VIRGIL

A rumor without a leg to stand on will get around some other way.

JOHN TUDOR

Lighten Up

Paul wrote: Jesus said to me, "My grace is sufficient for you, for My strength is made perfect in weakness." Therefore most gladly I will rather boast in my infirmities, that the power of Christ may rest upon me.
—2 Corinthians 12:9 NKJV

As a believer, you are supposed to strive for excellence in all you do. And no doubt you want to achieve excellence, knowing that it's attainable through the power God gives you and that it's a testimony to His activity in your life. A Christian who is known for adhering to a standard of excellence reflects well on the God he or she serves, so you try to do your best.

However, there's a hidden danger in your efforts to attain excellence, and that's the possibility that all your striving could spill over into the very undesirable area of perfectionism—the sense that anything short of perfection is unacceptable. That kind of thinking can be a killer. How can that be? After all, it sounds so positive. Shouldn't people strive to be perfect? The simple answer to that is no, mainly because it's a pointless goal. Only God is perfect; humans will never attain perfection.

But how can perfectionism kill? First, it destroys your peace of mind, because perfectionism always pushes you to do more or to be better or to adhere to some impossible standard of achievement. Perfectionism also ruins your emotional and mental health and is a major contributor to such disorders as chronic nervousness, anxiety, and depression. It kills your creativity, because you subconsciously believe that if you produce something that is imperfect, you are a failure. It threatens to damage your relationships, as you carry unattainably high standards over to others and drive them away from you in the process. It causes you to risk serious injury to your body by trying to be the perfect athlete. It kills your sheer enjoyment of life, because pleasure and relaxation don't fit your image of one who is striving for perfection. Fun becomes a burden, one more thing that must be done perfectly. Life becomes one long should, an existence characterized by duty and obligation. The life of a perfectionist is out of balance.

What's more, perfectionism can paralyze your spiritual growth—especially if you've been misinterpreting some key scriptures about perfection, like Romans 12:2. You've probably heard people quote this verse to encourage you to seek God's perfect will—which, of course, you should do. But some Christians get all bent out of shape over this verse, thinking that they can't make a move until they are absolutely certain that they positively know what God definitely wants them to do—before they even get out of bed in the morning. Whew! If you're one of those people, you need to get straightened out as soon as possible, first of all by realizing that finding God's will for your life is not a cosmic game of hide-and-seek. God isn't some kind of trickster, telling you only that you're hot or cold, forcing you to keep asking, "Am I getting warm?" He wants you to discover His will, but remember—perfect refers to His will, not to your attempts at discerning it. Relax and let it unfold before your eyes, as you focus on Him and walk in obedience.

If you still aren't convinced about the detrimental effects of perfectionism, consider this: If you expect to go to the perfect college, you'll never go. If you wait for the perfect job, you'll end up on welfare. If you hope to find the perfect mate, you'll never marry. God is so much kinder than to make you stress out over these things. He wants you to mature in your ability to trust Him, and He wants you to get rid of your fear of making a mistake that will ruin your life.

Get back to your original goal—maintaining a standard of excellence. You can accomplish that without getting twisted in knots. Lighten up and don't take your mistakes so seriously. Recognize your limitations and learn to say no. Stop trying to do everything flawlessly. Take time to have fun and enjoy yourself. Most of all, remember that you're human. No one—especially not God—expects you to be perfect or anything close to it. Take your perfectionist ways and transfer them to the only place they rightfully belong, in the hands of the only Perfect One.

I Will

Remember that only God is perfect. _____ yes _____ no

Trust God to reveal His will to me, in His own
way and His own time. _____ yes _____ no

Concentrate on excellence rather than perfection. _____ yes _____ no

Go easy on myself when I make a mistake. _____ yes _____ no

Lead a more balanced life. _____ yes _____ no

Realize how unhealthy perfectionism is. _____ yes _____ no

Things to Do

☐ Thank God that He doesn't expect you to be perfect.

☐ Give God your fear of making some monumental mistake.

☐ Write down what you can do to keep your standard of excellence
without turning it into perfectionism.

☐ List the various ways perfectionism can affect—or has affected—your
health.

☐ Isolate one activity in which you border on becoming an overachiever,
and develop a strategy for going easier on yourself in that area.

☐ Tackle something you've been afraid to do because you thought you
might mess up on it.

Things to Remember

All have sinned and fall short of the glory of God.

ROMANS 3:23 NKJV

Am I now seeking the favor of men, or of God? Or am I striving to please men? If I were still trying to please men, I would not be a bond-servant of Christ.

GALATIANS 1:10 NASB

It is the LORD's blessing that makes a person rich, and hard work adds nothing to it.

—PROVERBS 10:22 GOD'S WORD

When they continued asking Him, Jesus raised Himself up and said to them, "He who is without sin among you, let him throw a stone at her first."

JOHN 8:7–8 NKJV

As for God, His way is perfect; the word of the LORD is proven; He is a shield to all who trust in Him.

PSALM 18:30 NKJV

We know in part and we prophesy in part. But when that which is perfect has come, then that which is in part will be done away.

1 CORINTHIANS 13:9–10 NKJV

What has man for all his labor, and for the striving of his heart with which he has toiled under the sun?

ECCLESIASTES 2:22 NKJV

Have you lost your senses? After starting your Christian lives in the Spirit, why are you now trying to become perfect by your own human effort?

GALATIANS 3:3 NLT

You are complete in Him, who is the head of all principality and power.

COLOSSIANS 2:10 NKJV

Paul wrote: I take pleasure in infirmities, in reproaches, in needs, in persecutions, in distresses, for Christ's sake. For when I am weak, then I am strong.

2 CORINTHIANS 12:10 NKJV

If you wait for perfect conditions, you will never get anything done.

ECCLESIASTES 11:4 NLT

Perfectionism is the enemy of creation.

—JOHN UPDIKE

Better to do something imperfectly than to do nothing perfectly.

—ROBERT SCHULLER

Getting Some Downtime

It is vain for you to rise up early, to sit up late, to eat the bread of sorrows; for so He gives His beloved sleep.

—Psalm 127:2 NKJV

If you are like many teenagers, you stay up late at night, listening to music, talking on the phone, surfing the Internet, watching television, or studying. Before you know it, the alarm clock is nagging at you to get up, and once you get to school you spend all first period and half of second in a semicomatose condition. Eventually, sleep deprivation will catch up to you—either in your grades or by your mood. After a while your friends will start to walk the other way when they see your morning face coming.

Fortunately, you have a reliable mechanism—physical fatigue—that tells you when you need to start getting more sleep on a daily basis. But you also need another kind of rest, one that's less obvious. That kind of rest used to be called keeping the Sabbath, and your parents may still call it that. Lots of people misunderstand this gift from God; they get it confused with rules and regulations, or else they just ignore the whole idea. But God—who, by the way, based the notion of the Sabbath on personal experience—knew that if people were left to their own way of doing things, they would never take time out to just be.

The idea, of course, is to be in the presence of God for one day a week. Does that mean you have to spend all day in church? Or reading your Bible and praying? Not at all. It means that God is giving you an opportunity to break away from the routines of your life. Your whole day can become a prayer to Him, and in return, you can experience spiritual renewal and refreshment.

You may find you'll have to fight for your day of rest (sounds like a contradiction, doesn't it?). Life in the twenty-first century doesn't make the Sabbath rest come easily—you're surrounded by distractions or commitments that others schedule for you, seven days a week. Unfortunately, you may have already conditioned yourself to go for fairly long periods of time in a state of emotional, mental, and spiritual fatigue without realizing it. That's why it's important to schedule some Sabbath time, no matter how busy you are. In fact, if you insist that you don't have time to rest, you are putting forth a good argument for how much you need it. Start small, with a few hours of downtime each week. You may just discover what a great gift it is.

I Will

Realize that taking a Sabbath rest is a gift from God.   yes _____   no _____

Be thankful that God encourages me to take a break.   yes _____   no _____

Focus on the importance of spiritual refreshment.   yes _____   no _____

Get the amount of sleep I need each night.   yes _____   no _____

Give up the unnecessary things that interfere with
my need for rest.   yes _____   no _____

Recognize times when I'm emotionally, mentally, and
spiritually tired.   yes _____   no _____

Things to Do

☐ Read what Jesus said about the Sabbath in the Gospels. Get a firm
handle on it so no one can ever rob you of this gift by adding
rules to it.

☐ Thank God for wanting to spend time with you.

☐ Track your sleep pattern for a week; figure out how much sleep you
need and make that your nightly goal.

☐ Make a list of ways you can take a Sabbath rest (spend an afternoon
lying on a riverbank; posting a DO NOT DISTURB sign on your bedroom
door; sitting on a park bench).

☐ Choose one method on your list and take a Sabbath rest, starting with a
few hours. Keep your thoughts turned toward God.

Things to Remember

Return unto thy rest, O my soul; for the LORD hath dealt bountifully with thee.

PSALM 116:7 KJV

The LORD said to Moses, "You shall proclaim on the same day that it is a holy convocation to you. You shall do no customary work on it. It shall be a statute forever in all your dwellings throughout your generations."

LEVITICUS 23:21 NKJV

The LORD said, "I have satiated the weary soul, and I have replenished every sorrowful soul." After this I awoke and looked around, and my sleep was sweet to me, Jeremiah wrote.

JEREMIAH 31:25–26 NKJV

I fall asleep in peace the moment I lie down because you alone, O LORD, enable me to live securely.

PSALM 4:8 GOD'S WORD

Jesus said, "Take My yoke upon you and learn from Me, for I am gentle and lowly in heart, and you will find rest for your souls."

MATTHEW 11:29 NKJV

• •

Because God is the Ceaseless Worker, we can afford to stop, and to rest, and to commit to him the arrears in our work, as well as the work done.

ERIC S. ABBOTT

The time to relax is when you don't have time for it.

SIDNEY J. HARRIS

Persecution Plus

Moses said to all of Israel, "Be strong and of good courage, do not fear nor be afraid of them; for the Lord your God, He is the One who goes with you. He will not leave you nor forsake you."

—*Deuteronomy 31:6* NKJV

In survey after survey, rejection ranks near the top of the list of fears that people have. When you stop and think of all of the catastrophes and disasters that could have placed higher on those lists but didn't, you realize how deeply rejection affects people. Why people fear it so much is something of a mystery, because being rejected is as predictable as pretty much anything else in life.

In fact, if you were to meet ten new people today, it's almost a certainty that two of them will flat out reject you. But don't fear: Their rejection will be canceled out by the two people who will take to you immediately. The other six? Well, they won't think a whole lot about you one way or the other. And by the way, this works both ways: Of those ten new acquaintances, you'll probably accept two, reject two, and dismiss the other six. At least, that's what one psychiatrist claims, and he's studied all this a long time.

In any event, it's clear that you need to get used to being rejected, and even more so if you're a believer. The Bible comes right out and says that you'll face persecution, which is rejection with a mean streak. So now the ball is in your court: How will you handle the rejection that is certain to come your way? As always, the Bible offers lots of help

Your first defense in dealing with rejection is simply to expect it. Many fears are rooted in uncertainty, but this one is a given. In Matthew 10, Jesus tried to prepare His disciples for the kind of treatment they could expect—basically, the same kind He got. And you know what happened to Him! Of course, Jesus was speaking of those who would be rejected because of their association with Him. But even in your personal relationships, you need to realize that not everyone who pledges their undying devotion to you will actually keep that pledge. That's not to say that you shouldn't trust your close friends, but you shouldn't become so wrapped up in any one person that your entire well-being depends on their friendship.

Second, you need to be more concerned about pleasing God than pleasing anyone else. In essence, that's the defining quality of a true servant of Christ. The fear of having people reject them is one of the primary reasons why believers are reluctant to share their faith—or even to let others know that they're Christians! That's hardly exemplary conduct for someone who claims to be a follower of Jesus. Does God want you to share the good news of His salvation with other people? Of course He does. Should you avoid doing that because you're afraid of what people will think of you? Of course not. If you've counted the cost of discipleship (Luke 14:25–33), your priorities should already be in place, with pleasing God right at the top.

Finally, you need to continue to love other people in spite of the possibility of rejection. Paul was a great example of this. As a leader in the early church, sometimes he had to deal with an assortment of difficult situations, especially with the unruly church at Corinth. The things he had to do to bring order to the church didn't win him any popularity contests. But his heart remained "wide open" (2 Corinthians 6:11) to those who had closed their hearts to him, at least temporarily. Despite the rejection, he continued to open his heart to them and encouraged other believers to do the same.

As you read through different portions of the Bible, you'll find numerous references to rejection—mainly because of the many individuals and entire cultures that rejected God. But you'll also find the evidence of a merciful God who continued to love those who hated Him. And as usual, He expects you to imitate Him, which means He expects you to love those who hate you. Bless those who curse you, and pray for those who despise you— that's how Jesus put it in Matthew 5:44.

Oh yes, and don't forget to keep rejoicing. Even in the midst of persecution.

I Will

Desire to please God rather than man.

_____   _____

Share the gospel regardless of the reaction I get.

yes   no
_____   _____

Expect to be rejected.

yes   no
_____   _____

Love people even when they reject me.

yes   no
_____   _____

Realize that I don't accept everyone I meet either.

yes   no
_____   _____

Know that there is a cost to discipleship.

yes   no
_____   _____

Things to Do

☐ Thank God that He has promised never to abandon you.

☐ Ask God to forgive you for the times you've rejected people.

☐ Meditate on the persecution Jesus suffered on your behalf.

☐ Consciously forgive someone who has rejected you.

☐ Fearlessly share your faith with someone today.

☐ Think about what it means to be rejected and write in your journal about how it applies to your life.

Things to Remember

Jesus said, "Blessed are you when men hate you, and when they exclude you, and revile you, and cast out your name as evil, for the Son of Man's sake."

LUKE 6:22 NKJV

The LORD said, "Behold, I am going to deal at that time with all your oppressors, I will save the lame and gather the outcast, and I will turn their shame into praise and renown in all the earth."

ZEPHANIAH 3:19 NASB

The LORD will not cast off His people, nor will He forsake His inheritance.

—PSALM 94:14 NKJV

Blessed be God, because he has not rejected my prayer or removed his steadfast love from me.

PSALM 66:20 NRSV

We know that all things work together for good to those who love God, to those who are the called according to His purpose.

ROMANS 8:28 NKJV

Jesus strictly warned and commanded them to tell this to no one, saying, "The Son of Man must suffer many things, and be rejected by the elders and chief priests and scribes, and be killed, and be raised on the third day."

LUKE 9:21–22 NKJV

The LORD said, "I will make My dwelling among you, and My soul will not reject you."

LEVITICUS 26:11 NASB

Paul wrote: I am persuaded that neither death nor life, nor angels nor principalities nor powers, nor things present nor things to come, nor height nor depth nor any other created thing, shall be able to separate us from the love of God which is in Christ Jesus our Lord.

ROMANS 8:38–39 NKJV

Coming to Him as to a living stone, rejected indeed by men, but chosen by God and precious, you also, as living stones, are being built up a spiritual house, a holy priesthood, to offer up spiritual sacrifices acceptable to God through Jesus Christ.

1 PETER 2:4–5 NKJV

He is despised and rejected by men, a Man of sorrows and acquainted with grief. And we hid, as it were, our faces from Him; He was despised, and we did not esteem Him.

ISAIAH 53:3 NKJV

We keep going back, stronger, not weaker, because we will not allow rejection to beat us down. It will only strengthen our resolve. To be successful there is no other way.

—EARL G. GRAVES

False friends are like our shadow, keeping close to us while we walk in the sunshine, but leaving us the instant we cross into the shade.

—CHRISTIAN NEVELL BOVEE

Supersize It

In the multitude of words sin is not lacking, but he who restrains his lips is wise.

—Proverbs 10:19 NKJV

The truth, the whole truth, and nothing but the truth. Right? Your friends surround you, and the spotlight is shining right on you. You're in the middle of telling them this great story about—well, it hardly matters what it's about. You're clearly entertaining them. Suddenly, you get this bright idea that would make the story so much better. So you throw in a couple of details that aren't exactly true, but they sound great. No harm done, right?

Wrong. When you "supersize" your stories, you cross a line from fact into fiction, from truth into untruth. Calling it exaggeration may make it sound better, but it's still a form of lying. Unfortunately, this is a common lapse of integrity among Christians; the phrase "evangelistically speaking" is used in a cynical way to refer to the habit of inflating the number of people at an evangelistic event or the number of decisions for Christ that were logged. Maybe you've even been guilty of a little "evangelistic" exaggeration, thinking you could help out God a bit by adding a few dramatic but untrue touches when you tell others how He's been working in your life lately.

Well, God doesn't need anyone's help. What He needs is for His followers to be people of integrity, people whose word can be trusted. If you habitually exaggerate, you stand to lose your credibility, and that casts a shadow on your reputation as a Christian. How can you be a strong witness for Jesus if others cannot trust what you say? You can't. If you want to share the Good News, your word—your credibility—has to be as good as gold.

Think of it this way: You know you can take God at His word, so people should be able to take you at your word. They shouldn't have to wonder if what you're saying is really true or if you're just off again on another excursion into the land of tall tales. Let the truth of what you're saying stand on its own—you'll only weaken the impact by trying to prop up your words with lies.

When it comes right down to it, supersizing your stories really is a lot like supersizing your fast-food order; it sounds good, but the only thing you get more of is the stuff that's loaded with empty calories. Start downsizing your speech by making sure that every statement you make is true, and forget those bright ideas that sound so good. The truth always makes a better story.

I Will

Remember that God doesn't need me to
exaggerate to make Him sound better.   yes _____   no _____

Understand how important credibility is to my
reputation as a Christian.   yes _____   no _____

Trust God to help me keep my words pure.   yes _____   no _____

Commit myself to complete honesty in my speech.   yes _____   no _____

Realize that dramatic touches are nothing more
than lies.   yes _____   no _____

Focus on maintaining my integrity.   yes _____   no _____

Things to Do

☐ Confess the sins of exaggeration you've committed that God's Spirit
brings to your mind right now.

☐ Recall the last time you embellished on a story and figure out what
prompted you to exaggerate.

☐ Pray that God will help you to speak only the truth.

☐ Decide now that next time, you will resist the temptation to supersize
your stories.

☐ Skim a newspaper or magazine until you find an example of
exaggeration and think about how it affects the speaker's or writer's
credibility.

Things to Remember

Let no one deceive you with empty words, for because of these things the wrath of God comes on those who are disobedient.

EPHESIANS 5:6 NRSV

There is not a word on my tongue, but behold, O LORD, You know it altogether.

PSALM 139:4 NKJV

"Let him who glories glory in this, that he understands and knows Me, that I am the LORD, exercising lovingkindness, judgment, and righteousness in the earth. For in these I delight," says the LORD.

JEREMIAH 9:24 NKJV

Since you know that he cares, let your language show it. Don't add words like "I swear to God" to your own words. Don't show your impatience by concocting oaths to hurry up God. Just say yes or no. Just say what is true. That way, your language can't be used against you.

JAMES 5:12 THE MESSAGE

The boastful shall not stand in Your sight; You hate all workers of iniquity.

PSALM 5:5 NKJV

· ·

We always weaken everything we exaggerate.

JEAN-FRANÇOIS DE LA HARPE

Exaggeration is a blood relation to falsehood and nearly as blamable.

HOSEA BALLOU

Totally Awesome

Who is like You, O Lᴏʀᴅ, among the gods? Who is like You,
glorious in holiness, fearful in praises, doing wonders?
—Exodus 15:11 NKJV

Do you wonder how God reveals Himself to people
who don't have access to a Bible or who have never met a
Christian? Down through the centuries, people have
testified to their knowledge of God—and Jesus—through
the signs and wonders they observed in creation. For the
most part, these were people who lived close to nature
and recognized the unseen hand behind all that they
experienced. That, and God's Spirit working in their spirit,
was all they needed to recognize the same God you
worship.

The farther people get from a rural society, the harder
it is to see God with that same sense of wonder. But you
can do it, even if you live in a city. Instead of marveling at
the wonders of virtual reality, allow God's reality to
captivate you once in a while. Marvel at the colors in a
sunset or the playfulness of a dolphin (even if it's in an
aquarium) or the way a lizard scurries up a wall. Ancient

monastics and modern teachers have advised spiritual seekers and art students alike to study just one thing—a rock, a tree, a blade of grass—for a few hours or even a few weeks! Those who have done that say that they gained a profound appreciation for the Creator. It's a great way to keep your sense of wonder in shape.

All through your life, you'll meet people who will threaten to rob you of that sense of wonder. They're jaded, and they want jaded company. Don't go along with them. Take time, at least once in a while, to allow the incredible works of God—His works of creation as well as the works He performs in the lives of people—to stir your senses. Every answered prayer is something to marvel over, and every changed life is an awesome testimony to the power of God; to forget that is also to lose your sense of wonder.

The more intimately you get to know God and the more you let Him work in your life, the sooner you will come to realize that He alone is totally awesome. Getting to know Him is not at all like getting to know humans. When you open your eyes to the wonders He performs, God provides a never-ending source of fascination.

I Will

Realize that every life—including mine—is a
testimony to God.

Train myself to recognize the unseen hand of God
at work all around me.

Allow God to impress me every now and then.

Be thankful for the incredible world God has
given me.

Spend time with those who share my appreciation
for the wonders of creation.

Things to Do

☐ Ask God to open your eyes in a new way to the world around you.

☐ Take a tip from the monastics and for several hours study just one thing
God created.

☐ Read an overly familiar Bible story—perhaps the birth of Jesus—as if
you're reading it for the very first time.

☐ Make a list of the ways you would know God exists even if no one had
ever told you about Him.

☐ Meditate on Psalm 19 or another passage that testifies to the
awesomeness of God.

☐ Consciously go through one day determined to be more aware of God's
wonders. At the end of the day, write down what you discovered.

Things to Remember

The heavens keep telling the wonders of God, and the skies declare what he has done.

PSALM 19:1 CEV

The LORD asked Job, "Can you shout to the clouds and make it rain? Can you make lightning appear and cause it to strike as you direct it?"

JOB 38:34–35 NLT

They were all amazed, and they glorified God and were filled with fear, saying, "We have seen strange things today!"

LUKE 5:26 NKJV

Those living far away fear your wonders; where morning dawns and evening fades you call forth songs of joy.

PSALM 65:8 NIV

The men marveled, saying, "Who can this be, that even the winds and the sea obey Him?"

MATTHEW 8:27 NKJV

• •

Every object in nature is impressed with God's footsteps, and every day repeats the wonders of creation.

THOMAS GUTHRIE

A man who has lost his sense of wonder is a man dead.

WILLIAM OF SAINT THIERRY

Leader of the Pack

---

*Let no one despise your youth, but be an example to the
believers in word, in conduct, in love, in spirit, in faith, in
purity.* —*1 Timothy 4:12* NKJV

When it comes to role models, you've got two
considerations to keep in mind: being one and having one.
Whether you realize it or not, you are one and you have
at least one. That's why it's so important that you
understand what a role model is and how a role model
influences the lives of others.

People often talk of athletes and celebrities as role
models, but the reality is that a genuine role model is
someone actively involved in your everyday life, not some
distant superstar. Granted, a role model is the kind of
person you want to emulate, but a true role model has to
be someone you can relate to. It does little good to select
a basketball player as a role model if you're barely tall
enough to be allowed on the adult rides at Disney
World—unless what you're emulating is his character and
not his athletic skill. Even so, you'll soon realize that it's
the close-at-hand adults in your life—your parents,

teachers, youth leader—that will have the greatest effect on your character, because you're constantly observing the way they handle the nitty-gritty details of everyday life. That's a far cry from the media-filtered image that a celebrity wants you to see.

Make no mistake about it, you, too, are a role model, whether for a peer or a sibling or a kid in your neighborhood. No matter what you do, others, particularly younger others, are watching how you handle the ordinary details of everyday life as well. You are having an effect on them, whether for good or for bad. That's another reason why it's critical for you to understand that the words you speak cannot be called back and that the actions you take cannot be erased from the minds and imaginations of others.

Don't ever think that your life is so insignificant that you won't influence someone else. You not only affect the people around you now, but you will also affect generations to come, through your future children. As the saying goes, you may be the only Bible that some people read; the way you live your life stands as a silent witness to your faith in God. That's a daunting thought, but as always, God is right there to take the pressure off. As long as the overriding desire of your life is to please Him, then the influence you have on others can't help but be a positive one.

I Will

Trust God to give me the ability to be a positive
influence on others.   yes _____   no _____

Understand the influence that those involved in
my daily life are having on me.   yes _____   no _____

Remember that others are watching
everything I do.   yes _____   no _____

Be especially careful around younger kids who
may see me as a role model.   yes _____   no _____

Realize that my life may be the only Bible some
people read.   yes _____   no _____

Things to Do

☐ List the character qualities that you'd like to emulate and figure out who
in your life models those qualities.

☐ Take that same list and turn it into a set of goals for developing your
own character.

☐ Select a celebrity that you or your friends consider a role model.
Compare what you know about him or her with the character qualities
on your list.

☐ Read a classic on Jesus as the ultimate role model (such as The
Imitation of Christ by Thomas à Kempis, available at
<http://www.ccel.org/k/kempis/imitation/imitation.html>.

☐ Read about one "radical young believer" from the book Extreme Faith.

Things to Remember

Imitate me, just as I also imitate Christ.

1 CORINTHIANS 11:1 NKJV

In everything set [the young men] an example by doing
what is good. In your teaching show integrity, seriousness
and soundness of speech that cannot be condemned, so
that those who oppose you may be ashamed because they
have nothing bad to say about us.

TITUS 2:7–8 NIV

Therefore take up the whole armor of God, that you may
be able to withstand in the evil day, and having done all,
to stand.

EPHESIANS 6:13 NKJV

Paul wrote: Dear brothers, pattern your lives after mine
and notice who else lives up to my example.

PHILIPPIANS 3:17 TLB

Your word is a lamp to my feet and a light to my path.

PSALM 119:105 NKJV

• •

There is no power on earth that can neutralize the
influence of a high, simple, and useful life.

BOOKER T. WASHINGTON

Nothing is so contagious as an example. We never do great
good or evil without bringing about more of the same on
the part of others.

FRANÇOIS DE LA ROCHEFOUCAULD

Fair Play

Be kindly affectionate to one another with brotherly love, in honor giving preference to one another.

—Romans 12:10 NKJV

The best and most rewarding competition is that which you have with yourself, not others. But mention the word *competition*, and most people think of sports or the business world. And as a teenager, you're well aware of another brand of competition, the kind that stems from the normal need for attention. That's the kind that can get ugly really fast, as girls compete for the attention of a certain guy, or academic types vie for a scholarship reference from just the right teacher—or gangs contend for a certain piece of turf. That kind of competition locks you into an intense rivalry in which you view others as opponents rather than companions. Unlike healthy competitions, these personal battles ignore the rules of fair play.

The disciples weren't immune to this negative behavior. In one incident described in the Gospels, several of Jesus' followers were walking along and arguing about which one of them would be the greatest in the kingdom of God. Talk about misguided! When they realized that Jesus had overheard their dispute, they got quiet. Then He set them straight: "If anyone desires to be first, he shall be last of all and servant of all," He said in Mark 9:35, giving twenty-first century disciples something to think about as well.

God wants you to experience unity rather than rivalry with other people, especially other believers. Your loving relationship with other Christians is so important that it's one of the surest indications that you love God. While He was on earth, Jesus even prayed to the Father that His followers would be united, so the world would believe that God was the one who had sent Jesus (John 17:21).

All of this runs counter to the signals, and the outright messages, society sends your way. It also runs counter to your human nature. Under some circumstances, feeling competitive toward others can seem almost as natural as breathing, which is all the more reason why you have to take the words of Jesus to heart and fight like crazy to avoid competition in your personal relationships.

Make it your quest to outdo yourself, not others. Strive to do better—get a better grade, handle a situation in a more mature way—than you did last time. Play fair in your relationships by competing only with yourself. When you learn to focus on improving yourself, you'll be able to see others as companions on your journey through life, not as a field of opponents in a grueling marathon.

I Will

Remember that those who strive to be first in the kingdom will end up last.

_____ yes _____ no

Trust God to help me in those areas where I feel particularly competitive.

_____ yes _____ no

Seek to please God in the way I serve others.

_____ yes _____ no

Know that it is possible to turn competitors into companions.

_____ yes _____ no

Learn to see others as companions.

_____ yes _____ no

Concentrate on improving myself.

_____ yes _____ no

Things to Do

☐ Select one of the quotations on the facing page and write in your journal about how it applies to your life.

☐ Make a list of the ways you draw attention to yourself. Highlight the ones that involve unhealthy competition and resolve to eliminate those first.

☐ Choose someone you view as a rival (or a potential rival). Pray that he will succeed in the very area where you feel competitive toward him.

☐ Think of how you can outdo yourself. Then come up with a pressure-free game plan to accomplish it.

☐ Pray for unity with other believers.

Things to Remember

Everyone who competes for the prize is temperate in all things. Now they do it to obtain a perishable crown, but we for an imperishable crown.

1 CORINTHIANS 9:25 NKJV

If anyone competes as an athlete, he does not receive the victor's crown unless he competes according to the rules.

2 TIMOTHY 2:5 NIV

Jesus said, "That they all may be one, as You, Father, are in Me, and I in You; that they also may be one in Us, that the world may believe that You sent Me."

JOHN 17:21 NKJV

Then you will understand what is right and just and fair— every good course in life.

PROVERBS 2:9 GOD'S WORD

He is the Rock, His work is perfect; for all His ways are justice, a God of truth and without injustice; righteous and upright is He.

DEUTERONOMY 32:4 NKJV

....

Being part of an agenda beyond ourselves liberates us to complement each other rather than compete with each other.

JOSEPH STOWELL

Focus on competition has always been a formula for mediocrity.

DANIEL BURRUS

Deal with It

A friend loves at all times, and a brother is born for adversity.

—Proverbs 17:17 NKJV

Conflicts between siblings are as old as the first post—Garden of Eden society, the family of Adam and Eve. Sibling rivalry turned deadly right away, as Cain killed his brother, Abel, in a fit of jealous rage. In Luke 6, Jesus recommended—rather, commanded—a better way to deal with those people, like siblings, who irritate the daylights out of you: Love them, do good to them, bless them, pray for them. Turn the other cheek so they can hit that one too. Let them steal from you, and give them the shirt off your back. Don't ask them to return what they've taken from you.

That list probably bugs you, at least a little bit. This isn't easy. You might want to note that Jesus gave no guarantee that the other person's behavior will ever change. He's interested in the changes these actions will make in your character. So don't look for your siblings to act nicer—but then again, don't be all that surprised if the atmosphere at home starts to get a bit more pleasant.

If you don't have a sister or brother, you'll find that these principles also apply to other relationships in your life. In some families, cousins are practically siblings, and the dynamics among cousins can escalate into tension-creating situations similar to what you find among siblings. Like a sister or brother, your cousins will always be related to you, and you share a bond that's not based on preference but on family. God places a great deal of importance on family; it's no accident that you were born into a particular clan. In large part, your personality and character are shaped by the early influences in your life, so you'd do well to learn to appreciate your relatives and treat them in a godly way.

Friends may come and go, but your family will always be your family. As you get older, and especially after you have children of your own, you'll begin to recognize how valuable your family relationships are. Start to treat your siblings as valuable people now, while you're still living at home. Practice kindness and courtesy toward your sister, your brother, your cousin. Look out for them; don't tease or make fun of them, and don't let others do it either. The love you express to your family through your actions will reap untold benefits now and in the future.

I Will

Realize that God is interested in changing my
character through my interactions with others.   yes ___   no ___

Believe that Jesus really does want me to treat
others as He described in Luke 6.   yes ___   no ___

Appreciate the family God has placed me in.   yes ___   no ___

Treat my siblings and cousins with kindness.   yes ___   no ___

Place a high value on the individual members of
my family.   yes ___   no ___

Defend my siblings or other relatives and always
speak highly of them.   yes ___   no ___

Things to Do

☐ Thank God for each person in your family, by name.

☐ Identify the main reasons for conflict with your siblings, admit your
part in them, and write down what you can do to change.

☐ Read Luke 6 as if Jesus intended for you to take His words seriously.

☐ Who bugs you the most in your family? Make a list of that person's
good qualities.

☐ Give your brother or sister or cousin something of value to you, with no
strings attached. Make sure you give it out of love and not obligation.

☐ Bless the members of your family by asking God to bless them in some
special and specific way.

Things to Remember

Whoever loves a brother or sister lives in the light, and in such a person there is no cause for stumbling.

1 JOHN 2:10 NRSV

Behold, how good and how pleasant it is for brethren to dwell together in unity!

PSALM 133:1 NKJV

Jesus said, "Whoever does what God wants is my brother and sister and mother."

MARK 3:35 GOD'S WORD

Jesus said, "The glory which You gave Me I have given them, that they may be one just as We are one: I in them, and You in Me; that they may be made perfect in one, and that the world may know that You have sent Me, and have loved them as You have loved Me."

JOHN 17:22–23 NKJV

May the God of patience and comfort grant you to be like-minded toward one another, according to Christ Jesus.

ROMANS 15:5 NKJV

A brother is a friend provided by nature.

LEGOUVE PEREX

There is no friend like a sister in calm or stormy weather; to cheer one on the tedious way, to fetch one if one goes astray, to lift one if one totters down, to strengthen whilst one stands.

CHRISTINA ROSSETTI

Gift in Disguise

Do not be deceived, God is not mocked; for whatever a man sows, that he will also reap. For he who sows to his flesh will of the flesh reap corruption, but he who sows to the Spirit will of the Spirit reap everlasting life.
—Galatians 6:7–8 NKJV

If you're not familiar with the story of David and Bathsheba, you might want to take a look at it. It's found in 2 Samuel 11 and 12, and it speaks volumes about the consequences of sin. Briefly, the story goes like this: David notices this woman, Bathsheba, who lives near the palace, and he begins to lust after her. Problem is, she's married. But he's the king, and he generally can get what he wants. So he gets her—and gets her pregnant. Her husband, Uriah, has been off at war, so David sends for him, thinking that Uriah will sleep with Bathsheba. That way, when her pregnancy is discovered, no one will be the wiser; they'll think the baby is Uriah's.

But Uriah turns out to be a principled man—how can he justify engaging in pleasure when the nation is engaged in battle? He makes the mistake of avoiding Bathsheba, so David sends him to the front lines, all but ensuring his death. Uriah is killed, and David takes Bathsheba as his wife. When he is finally convicted of his sin—through the courageous kindness of a man named Nathan—David confesses his sin, repents, and receives God's merciful forgiveness. End of story? No. Look at the consequences of David's sin: Uriah is dead, as is the baby David fathered with Bathsheba. And David's family suffered because of his sin: His daughter, Tamar, was raped by Amnon (her half-brother); his son Absalom killed Amnon; Absalom led an uprising against David and was also eventually killed. According to Nathan, all of this happened because of what David did.

That ought to make you think about the consequences of sin. Even though David was forgiven, he still had to face the tragic events that resulted from caving in to his lustful desires. To his credit, David accepted full responsibility and sought to restore his relationship with God—and he relied on God to help him make the right choices during the turbulent times that followed. The consequence of his sin was a gift that kept his heart turned toward God.

Like David, you need to accept complete responsibility for your sin—along with the consequences. Thinking about those consequences ahead of time can save you a truckload of heartache and trouble in the future. Sin is seldom the isolated act it appears to be; a single act of sin can affect countless people and a host of future decisions. If David could have seen into the future, he no doubt would have hightailed it back into the palace and never stolen another glance at Bathsheba.

Avoiding sin is naturally the best deterrent to suffering

painful consequences. By allowing God to change the desires of your heart, limiting your exposure to tempting opportunities, and exercising self-control when you are confronted with sin, you can avoid following in David's misguided footsteps and possibly taking a lot of other people with you.

Everything you do—even those things that aren't sinful—carries implications. Sometimes you can do more harm than good even when you think you're doing the right thing. Peter did that, as did the Galatian church, and they both got quite a talking to from Paul. In their zeal, they had placed pressure on new believers and added legalistic rules to the gospel. Paul set them straight, but there's no telling how many potential converts were turned off before he got wind of the problem.

Learning to think before you act is not a bad habit to get into. Neither is asking yourself that once-trendy-but-still-valid question, "What would Jesus do?" You can't expect to accurately predict what will happen, but by fast-forwarding your thoughts into the future, your imagination can do a pretty good job of offering up a series of possible scenarios. By looking to Jesus as the ideal example of living right, you should have a lot less concern about the consequences of the decisions you make.

Because of the disobedience of Adam and Eve in the Garden of Eden, we live in a sinful world. Because of the obedience of Christ on the cross, we will have a sin-free eternity. The consequences of those two events affected billions of people and the decisions they made.

I Will

Ask "What would Jesus do?" when I'm not sure
how to decide.   yes   no

Realize that everything I do has implications.   yes   no

Accept full responsibility for my actions.   yes   no

Learn to think before I act.   yes   no

Avoid every opportunity for sin that I
possibly can.   yes   no

Understand that I can do harm even when I think
I'm doing something right.   yes   no

Things to Do

☐ Ask God to help you think about the consequences of your actions
before you act.

☐ Read Daniel 6 from the perspective of Daniel's obedience.

☐ Read Acts 5:1–11 to discover the consequences of Ananias's and
Sapphira's disobedience.

☐ Mentally replay your day to see how the decisions you made affected
the way the day went.

☐ Pray for someone whose poor choices have had negative consequences
in your life.

Things to Remember

God saw how corrupt the earth had become, for all the people on earth had corrupted their ways. So God said to Noah, "I am going to put an end to all people, for the earth is filled with violence because of them. I am surely going to destroy both them and the earth."

GENESIS 6:12–13 NIV

I, the Lord, search the heart, I test the mind,
Even to give every man according to his ways,
According to the fruit of his doings.

JEREMIAH 17:10 NKJV

Beloved, if our heart does not condemn us, we have confidence toward God. And whatever we ask we receive from Him, because we keep His commandments and do those things that are pleasing in His sight.

—1 JOHN 3:21–22 NKJV

To Adam, God said, "Because you listened to your wife and ate the fruit when I told you not to, I have placed a curse upon the soil. All your life you will struggle to extract a living from it."

GENESIS 3:17 TLB

Peter said to Simon, "Your money perish with you, because you thought that the gift of God could be purchased with money! You have neither part nor portion in this matter, for your heart is not right in the sight of God."

ACTS 8:20–21 NKJV

The wages of sin is death, but the gift of
God is eternal life in Christ Jesus our Lord.

ROMANS 6:23 NKJV

Jesus said, "He who receives a prophet in
the name of a prophet shall receive a
prophet's reward; and he who receives a
righteous man in the name of a righteous
man shall receive a righteous man's reward.
And whoever in the name of a disciple gives
to one of these little ones even a cup of cold
water to drink, truly I say to you, he shall
not lose his reward."

MATTHEW 10:41–42 NASB

Be sure to give to [the poor] without any
hesitation. When you do this, the Lord your
God will bless you in everything you work
for and set out to do.

DEUTERONOMY 15:10 GOD'S WORD

Daniel said, "My God sent his angel to shut
the lions' mouths so that they would not
hurt me, for I have been found innocent in
his sight. And I have not wronged you, Your
Majesty." The king was overjoyed and
ordered that Daniel be lifted from the den.
Not a scratch was found on him because he
had trusted in his God.

DANIEL 6:22–23 NLT

Sooner or later
everyone sits
down to a
banquet of
consequences.

—ROBERT LOUIS
STEVENSON

Every act is an
act of self-
sacrifice.
When you
choose anything
you reject
everything else.

—G. K. CHESTERSON

The Singing Heart

Rejoice in the Lord always. Again I will say, rejoice!
—*Philippians 4:4* NKJV

Some Christians seem to be pretty somber. What's up with that? Joy is supposed to be one of the hallmarks of the Christian life. Over and over again the Bible tells God's people to Rejoice! Sing with joy and gladness! Make a joyful noise! Nowhere does it suggest walking around with a long face, looking pious and serious. In fact, Jesus had nothing but harsh words for the Pharisees and other religious types whose grim and sour expressions turned people away from the living God.

The problem of the Pharisees—both ancient and modern-day types—is that they've never had a genuine, life-changing encounter with the Lord. If they had, they would be experiencing a joy that nothing could touch. The kind of joy that flows from a life in relationship with God is so different from happiness, which can be affected by circumstances. The joy God gives is utterly indestructible. Job, a guy who lost everything and was afflicted with all kinds of physical problems to boot, talked of finding joy in "unrelenting pain." Now there's a type of joy that survived the worst imaginable circumstances.

Look at the parables of Jesus and the images He used to describe the kingdom of God. He spoke of heaven as being like a banquet or a feast—and He didn't mean any kind of formal, stuffy affair either. In His time, a feast would have been one rollicking party. Even at the Last Supper, a serious meal if ever there was one, He spoke of overflowing joy. The reality is, you cannot separate joy from Jesus. If you truly have Jesus in your life, you have joy as well.

If you're not experiencing this kind of joy in your life, you first need to make sure you're in right relation with Jesus. Have you surrendered everything to Him and turned control of your life over to Him? If so—if you have accepted the gift of His salvation—ask Him to restore the joy of that gift to you. As you wait on Him, meditate on these two aspects of your new life: the sin He saved you from, and the incredible and awesome gifts He's given you, starting with the joyful hope of your inheritance, both on earth and in heaven. Let the joy that begins to bubble to the surface seep far down into your heart, to a place where nothing—no person, no circumstances, no event—can ever touch it. Then sing for joy!

I Will

Meditate on the incredible gifts God has given me.   yes ____ no. ____

Realize that if I truly have Jesus, then I will
experience joy.   yes ____ no ____

Rejoice in the Lord always!   yes ____ no ____

Understand that true joy is not affected by
circumstances.   yes ____ no ____

Allow the joy I feel to seep down into my spirit
and become a permanent part of my life.   yes ____ no ____

Know that it is impossible to separate joy
from Jesus   yes ____ no ____

Things to Do

☐ Spend some time thinking about the connection between joy and the hope you have in Christ. Write about that connection in your journal.

☐ Read how Jeremiah literally "ingested" joy in Jeremiah 15.

☐ Decide to have a day of untouchable joy; don't let anything rob you of your joy for one entire day.

☐ Sing to the Lord! Even if you have to sing a muffled song into your pillow, praise Him in joyful song.

☐ Look up joy using an online Bible search. List the accompanying action words (like shout and sing), then do those things as a form of worship.

Things to Remember

You have turned for me my mourning into dancing; You have put off my sackcloth and clothed me with gladness, to the end that my glory may sing praise to You and not be silent. O LORD my God, I will give thanks to you forever.

PSALM 30:11–12 NKJV

This is the day the Lord has made; we will rejoice and be glad in it.

PSALM 118:24 NKJV

My lips shall greatly rejoice when I sing to You, and my soul, which You have redeemed.

PSALM 71:23 NKJV

Shout with joy to the LORD, O earth! Worship the LORD with gladness. Come before him, singing with joy.

PSALM 100:1–2 NLT

The angel said to them, "Do not be afraid; for see—I am bringing you good news of great joy for all the people: to you is born this day in the city of David a Savior, who is the Messiah."

LUKE 2:10–11 NRSV

Those who bring sunshine into the lives of others cannot keep it from themselves.

SIR JAMES M. BARRIE

Joy is the feeling of grinning on the inside.

MELBA COLGROVE

Let's Get Real

> Therefore, putting away lying, "Let each one of you speak truth with his neighbor," for we are members of one another.
>
> —Ephesians 4:25 NKJV

Imagine what it would be like if you went to school tomorrow and discovered that you didn't recognize a single person. A few of your friends might seem a bit familiar, but they just didn't look the same. You'd feel as if you were dreaming, or were having a nightmare, or were the victim of some cruel hoax. But that imaginary scene at your school is what life would be like if you and everyone else removed their masks for a day.

Everyone wears a mask—the image they want others to see. What does yours look like? If it looks pretty much like the real you, you're among the minority. Many people wear masks that bear little resemblance to the real person behind it. What makes their lives so sad is that in their efforts to put on a good face for other people, they destroy any possibility of genuine fellowship with the very people they hope to impress.

By pretending to be someone or something you're not, you are undermining the work of God in your life. He made you the way you are. He loves you the way you are, but other people can't. How can they, if you never show them the real you? How will you ever know if their love and acceptance is genuine? If all they ever see is this phony image you've been presenting, you will never have the confidence of knowing that they accept you for who you really are.

Presenting a false image is a form of dishonesty, one that deceives other people and destroys your self-esteem. It's also among the greatest hindrances to open fellowship among Christians. Jesus came not only to reconcile humanity to God but also to reconcile person to person. When you place a false image between your true self and your fellow believers, you build a barrier.

Let people see the real you. Make yourself transparent and vulnerable to other Christians, even though it means that you'll run the risk of getting hurt. Honor the work of God in your life by stripping away the mask—or the many masks—you've been wearing. You'll become more approachable, more accessible, and more likable to others. And you might start to like yourself a little bit more as well.

I Will

Realize that I am undermining God's creation when
I try to be something I'm not.   yes _____   no _____

Show my real self to other people.   yes _____   no _____

Appreciate the person I am inside.   yes _____   no _____

Recognize those times when I am most likely to
put on a mask.   yes _____   no _____

Make myself vulnerable and transparent to other
believers.   yes _____   no _____

Try to get to know the real person behind the
mask another person is wearing.   yes _____   no _____

Things to Do

☐ Ask God to reveal to you the various masks you wear (such as a
"perfect Christian" mask).

☐ Hand over to God your fear of exposing the real you.

☐ Ask God to give you the strength to drop your masks and be the person
He made you to be.

☐ Ask yourself what's the worst that could happen if you removed your
masks.

☐ Read Acts 2:42–47 for a glimpse at how the early believers
fellowshipped with each other.

Things to Remember

He who would love life and see good days, let him refrain his tongue from evil, and his lips from speaking deceit.

1 PETER 3:10 NKJV

As long as my breath is in me and the spirit of God is in my nostrils, my lips will not speak falsehood, and my tongue will not utter deceit.

JOB 27:3–4 NRSV

Jesus said, "You shall know the truth, and the truth shall make you free."

JOHN 8:32 NKJV

David wrote: He who works deceit shall not dwell within my house; he who tells lies shall not continue in my presence.

PSALM 101:7 NKJV

A righteous man hates lying, but a wicked man is loathsome and comes to shame.

PROVERBS 13:5 NKJV

No man, for any considerable period, can wear one face to himself, and another to the multitude, without finally getting bewildered as to which may be true.

NATHANIEL HAWTHORNE

The easiest thing to be in the world is you. The most difficult thing to be is what other people want you to be. Don't let them put you in that position.

LEO BUSCAGLIA

No One's Looking

Lord, who may abide in Your tabernacle? Who may dwell in Your holy hill? He who walks uprightly, and works righteousness, and speaks the truth in his heart.

—Psalm 15:1–2 NKJV

God's Spirit talks to you through your conscience. Consider this scenario: It's late, you've had a rough day, and you're mindlessly chatting away with your buddies over the Internet. You get distracted by a pop-up window and just as mindlessly click on an innocuous-looking link. That's when your eyes just about pop out of your head. The image that appears is... indescribable in print. You quickly try to close the window, and six more like it suddenly appear on the screen. As you start to close each window, you find that your "clicker" is losing steam. You're not as quick at closing those windows as you were at first. But it's OK; there's no real harm done. No one's looking, right? Right?

Wrong, of course. For one thing, you are. You're looking at pictures that appeal to your worst instincts, and your conscience is sending out danger signals. And God is looking. He's not going to strike you down—though He has been known to do that kind of thing—but He is grieving at your willful sin. He's not holding you accountable for seeing that first image, but as for the ones that followed—well, that's another story. And that's the heart of unethical behavior—engaging in willful sin, particularly under circumstances that make it unlikely that you'll get caught.

In a single day, you may have dozens of occasions to make ethical decisions, most of which you handle without much thought. Maybe your guidance counselor has left you alone in her office for five minutes, just enough time for you to take a peek at some juicy files. But you don't even think twice about that—and you've scored an ethical victory without even realizing it.

Your conscience is your closest ally in your efforts to live an ethical life, because it's through your conscience that God's Spirit lets you know when you're about to cross over into questionable or dangerous territory. Think of the way your conscience has operated up until now. Has it ever given you wholehearted permission to sin along with a guarantee that you wouldn't be found out? No. Your conscience doesn't wink at you and look the other way so you can do something you know is wrong.

Become a God-pleaser by choosing to do right whenever you're confronted with an ethical dilemma—even when you think no one's looking. As you well know, someone always is.

I Will

Thank God for His mercy when I've made bad
decisions in the past.

yes _____ no _____

Realize that the Bible offers clear guidance for
godly behavior.

yes _____ no _____

Trust the Spirit of God to lead me to make ethical
decisions.

yes _____ no _____

Do the right thing, even in private.

yes _____ no _____

Pay attention to what my conscience is telling me.

yes _____ no _____

Think less about getting caught and more about
pleasing God.

yes _____ no _____

Things to Do

☐ Make a commitment to God to adhere to a biblical standard of ethical
behavior. Write it down.

☐ Meditate on the psalms that deal with ethical behavior,
like Psalms 1, 15, and 37.

☐ Think back over the past week and mentally assess how you handled
questionable circumstances.

☐ Prepare a defense against situation ethics—the belief that an action can
be either right or wrong depending on the situation.

☐ Ask God to forgive you for the times you have willfully disregarded
your conscience.

Things to Remember

Let integrity and uprightness preserve me, for I wait for You.

PSALM 25:21 NKJV

If we forgot the name of our God or stretched out our hands to pray to another god, wouldn't God find out, since he knows the secrets in our hearts?

PSALM 44:20–21 GOD'S WORD

When Gentiles, who do not have the law, by nature do things in the law, these, although not having the law, are a law to themselves, who show the work of the law written in their hearts, their conscience also bearing witness, and between themselves their thoughts accusing or else excusing them.

ROMANS 2:14–15 NKJV

Create in me a clean heart, O God, and renew a steadfast spirit in me.

PSALM 51:10 NKJV

O Lord, You have searched me and known me. You know my sitting down and my rising up; you understand my thought afar off.

PSALM 139:1–2 NKJV

• •

Evangelical faith without Christian ethics is a travesty on the gospel.

V. RAYMOND EDMAN

Let us raise a standard to which the wise and honest can repair; the rest is in the hands of God.

GEORGE WASHINGTON

Dissed

Jesus said, "When you are invited, go and sit down in the lowest place, so that when he who invited you comes he may say to you, 'Friend, go up higher.' Then you will have glory in the presence of those who sit at the table with you."

—Luke 14:10 NKJV

Respect, honor, and esteem flow naturally from a heart tuned to God. People been dissing you lately? You say they're not showing you any respect? You're certainly not alone! The habit of treating others with respect has taken a nosedive in recent decades, but thankfully, it hasn't disappeared altogether. And you can be on the cutting edge of restoring this habit to daily life, because you have the inside track on what it means to show respect to others.

The words *respect*, *honor*, and *esteem* are all over the pages of your Bible. You can look those words up in any dictionary and find a lot of abstract definitions, or you can remember these simple guidelines for showing respect: Treat individuals courteously, submit to authority, and give reverence to God. Now that you know what to do, you need to know how to do it.

How can you treat individuals courteously? You don't need to read a book on etiquette to figure this out. When it comes to people, respect involves placing another person's needs and comfort and wishes ahead of your own. It means moving aside so they can get ahead, both literally and figuratively. It includes listening to what they have to say without dismissing their ideas in advance. It entails little things like holding a door open for another person and big things like always speaking well of others. It consists of giving credit where credit is due, recognizing someone publicly for a job well done, extending kindness to a stranger, and never failing to thank someone for even the smallest gesture of kindness on their part. Respectful acts toward individuals come in so many varieties that you'll never get bored with them.

How can you submit to authority? Right now, you're probably still under the authority of your parents, as well as the authority of other adults such as teachers and bosses. Treat them courteously, and be obedient to them—not only in your actions but also in your spirit. You're at a time in your life when the government will soon be making more demands of you, and you need to be ready to submit to governmental authority as well. If you drive, you already have a taste of what that means, not only in the rules of the road that you're expected to follow but also in the paperwork you have to fill out, tests you need to pass, and fees you're required to pay. (If you own a car, double all that, and throw in mandatory insurance coverage!)

Submitting to the government is more than following a long

list of rules and regulations, though. For you as a believer, it means supporting your governing officials, at all levels, in prayer. They need God's guidance to make the wise decisions you're hoping they'll make. But never forget this: When any authority demands that you do something that is in conflict with a clear and unmistakable command of God, that's the point where your submission ends. In all matters, you must obey God—and not any human authority.

That's how you give reverence to God: by obeying Him and giving Him first place in your life. By loving Him, worshiping Him, praising Him. You honor God when you give Him the credit for His work in your life, when you introduce others to Him, when you consider of greatest importance those things that are important to Him. You show respect for Him by loving other people and by taking care of His creation.

To see the principle of respect toward individuals, authority, and God at work in one place, you need look no further than the short book of Philemon, which you'll find right before Hebrews. Paul, who is often maligned—OK, dissed—by modern-day readers for being brash, wrote it. In this short letter, Paul showed immense kindness toward a former slave, respect for his former master, and honor for God in the way he handled the return of the slave to his master. It's a textbook example of tactfulness.

Respect, honor, and esteem flow from a heart completely given over to God. You cannot honor God without honoring other people and the authorities placed over you. By becoming a model of respectful behavior, you bring even greater honor to the God you serve.

I Will

Understand that God has placed authorities over me.

yes _no_

Know that God is my ultimate authority.

yes _no_

Give reverence to God.

yes _no_

Consider people with respect.

yes _no_

Appreciate the kindness others extend to me.

yes _no_

Focus on the way I treat others instead of the way they treat me.

yes _no_

Things to Do

☐ Honor God today by publicly giving Him credit for the things He has done for you.

☐ Read the book of Philemon and learn from Paul's example.

☐ Ask God for creative ideas to show respect to others.

☐ In every church, at least one person does some kind of thankless, unrecognized job. Thank that person!

☐ The next time an elderly person enters the room, boldly stand up. (It's biblical.)

☐ Get together with some of your friends and devise a plan to honor your youth group leader or a favorite teacher.

Things to Remember

Sanctify the Lord God in your hearts, and always be ready to give a defense to everyone who asks you a reason for the hope that is in you, with meekness and fear; having a good conscience, that when they defame you as evildoers, those who revile your good conduct in Christ may be ashamed.

1 PETER 3:15–16 NKJV

The LORD said, "Rise in the presence of the aged, show respect for the elderly and revere your God."

LEVITICUS 19:32 NIV

Receive him therefore in the Lord with all gladness, and hold such men in esteem.

—PHILIPPIANS 2:29 NKJV

Give everyone what you owe him: If you owe taxes, pay taxes; if revenue, then revenue; if respect, then respect; if honor, then honor.

ROMANS 13:7 NIV

We urge you, brethren, to recognize those who labor among you, and are over you in the Lord and admonish you, and to esteem them very highly in love for their work's sake. Be at peace among yourselves.

1 THESSALONIANS 5:12–13 NKJV

Honor all people. Love the brotherhood. Fear God. Honor the king.

1 PETER 2:17 NKJV

Therefore the LORD God of Israel says: "I said indeed that your house and the house of your father would walk before Me forever." But now the LORD says: "Far be it from Me; for those who honor Me I will honor, and those who despise Me shall be lightly esteemed."

1 SAMUEL 2:30 NKJV

The wise will inherit honor, but fools display dishonor.

PROVERBS 3:35 NASB

A man's pride will bring him low, but the humble in spirit will retain honor.

PROVERBS 29:23 NKJV

The fear of the LORD teaches a man wisdom, and humility comes before honor.

PROVERBS 15:33 NIV

Paul wrote: Titus cares for you more than ever when he remembers the way you listened to him and welcomed him with such respect and deep concern.

2 CORINTHIANS 7:15 NLT

There is no respect for others without humility in one's self.

—HENRI FRÉDÉRIC AMIEL

Respect is love in plain clothes.

—FRANKIE BYRNE

Catch Up with You Later

Let us lay aside every weight, and the sin which so easily ensnares us, and let us run with endurance the race that is set before us. —Hebrews 12:1 NKJV

Procrastinating is a form of putting off good. Perhaps you have a paper due next week, but you figure you can whip it out in one night. Your parents have been on your case about applying for an after-school job, but this week looks really busy, and next week you've got that paper due, so it looks like you won't be employed any time soon. Oh, and you've been meaning to look up those scriptures your youth group leader encouraged you to memorize ages ago, but maybe you'll be able to get to that sometime after you finish your paper for school and you get that job you haven't applied for yet.

Sound familiar? The details may not be the same, but there's a pretty good chance that the tendency to put things off characterizes your day-to-day routine. It's another normal aspect of human behavior, especially when it comes to doing hard or unpleasant tasks. Maybe putting things off is an indication of laziness, but let's put a positive spin on it. Your reasons for procrastinating may be more noble than that. Perhaps you have such high standards that you're afraid you'll do poorly on the paper or not get the job or lose your ability to memorize things.

There's good news for you, either way. You can conquer procrastination, in one easy step! That's right! How? Just get the job done. Not as easy as you expected? Well, it's a whole lot easier than waiting till the last minute and stressing big time over something that could have been done weeks earlier.

The tasks you have to accomplish will not simply disappear into the misty realm of Tomorrowland. They'll still be there on the deadline day, and you'll still have to get them done. The longer you put them off, the more time you'll spend worrying about them. Your anxiety level will increase, and soon you'll feel overwhelmed. You need to just get started. Remember, there's no law against finishing that paper early, even if you just let it lie around and gather dust until the due date.

While it's important not to let tasks accumulate, it's even more important not to put off the genuinely important things in life—like calling a grandparent or other relative who has made a significant difference in your life or sending a thank-you note to someone who has done something special for you. When your genuinely good intentions fail to translate into specific actions, you're left with a stockpile of kindnesses that never made their way into the lives of others. They are blessings in name only.

What you need is a game plan to overcome your tendency to procrastinate. As with everything, it helps to go to God first. Talking this over with God and admitting that you have a problem in this area will make you more sensitive to the promptings of His Spirit when you encounter a situation or assignment that you'd like to put on the back burner. He'll not only remind you of the pitfalls involved in putting it off, but He'll also surprise you with creative ideas for getting it out of the way quickly.

God knows your temperament better than anyone does. He knows why you procrastinate, and He knows how you can conquer the habit. (You probably also know, but you may need a little divine nudge!) Are you the kind of person who likes keeping a to-do list, or does that idea drive you crazy? Maybe you love all the bells and whistles on your computer, and what would get you moving is some cool software that serves up electronic reminders along with your favorite MP3 files. You might be the type who likes sticky notes all over the place, especially if they're the black paper/gel pen variety. Whatever. Just don't put off figuring out the best way to deal with your procrastination!

The Bible says that you should never withhold good when it is in your power to give it (Proverbs 3:27–28). Often, the things you do procrastinate about involve withholding good from others. By becoming determined to immediately tackle the tasks at hand, you can be a blessing to God, other people, and even yourself.

I Will

Be aware of the promptings of God's Spirit when
He's telling me to do something—now.

yes _____ _no_ _____

Get started on tasks instead of putting them off.

yes _____ _no_ _____

Not withhold good from others when I have the
power to offer it.

yes _____ _no_ _____

Be aware of things I can do to help myself
conquer the habit of procrastination.

yes _____ _no_ _____

Realize the stressful toll procrastination takes on
my life.

yes _____ _no_ _____

Things to Do

☐ Ask God to make you sensitive to His nudges when you're tempted to
procrastinate.

☐ Find the best method (to-do list, sticky notes, high-tech gizmo) for you
to bring your tasks under control.

☐ Take one routine task you tend to put off (like homework) and create a
daily schedule for getting it done.

☐ Write a thank-you note to someone today—surely there's at least one
you've been putting off!

☐ What's the biggest task looming ahead of you? On paper, break it down
into smaller segments and get started on the first stage.

Things to Remember

We desire that each one of you show the same diligence to the full assurance of hope until the end, that you do not become sluggish, but imitate those who through faith and patience inherit the promises.

HEBREWS 6:11–12 NKJV

The hand of the diligent will rule, but the lazy man will be put to forced labor.

PROVERBS 12:24 NKJV

Because of laziness the building decays, and through idleness of hands the house leaks.

—ECCLESIASTES 10:18 NKJV

Not lagging in diligence, fervent in spirit, serving the Lord.

ROMANS 12:11 NKJV

"This is what the LORD of Armies says: These people say it's not the right time to rebuild the house of the LORD." Then the LORD spoke his word through the prophet Haggai. He said, "Is it time for you to live in your paneled houses while this house lies in ruins?"

HAGGAI 1:2–4 GOD'S WORD

Moses said, "The LORD will command the blessing on you in your storehouses and in all to which you set your hand, and He will bless you in the land which the LORD your God is giving you."

DEUTERONOMY 28:8 NKJV

When you make a vow to God, do not delay fulfilling it; for he has no pleasure in fools. Fulfill what you vow.

ECCLESIASTES 5:4 NRSV

He who has a slack hand becomes poor; but the hand of the diligent makes rich.

PROVERBS 10:4 NKJV

I will hurry, without lingering, to obey your commands.

PSALM 119:60 NLT

Do not withhold good from those who deserve it, when it is in your power to act. Do not say to your neighbor, "Come back later; I'll give it tomorrow"—when you now have it with you.

PROVERBS 3:27–28 NIV

The greatest amount of wasted time is the time not getting started.

—DAWSON TROTMAN

Putting off an easy thing makes it hard, and putting off a hard one makes it impossible.

—GEORGE H. LONMER

CRITICISM

Zipped Lips

Do not speak evil of one another, brethren. He who speaks evil of a brother and judges his brother, speaks evil of the law and judges the law. But if you judge the law, you are not a doer of the law but a judge. There is one Lawgiver, who is able to save and to destroy. Who are you to judge another?

—*James 4:11–12 NKJV*

Critic or criticizer? You had a really great time at a concert. You and your friends blew all your money on tickets and food, but it was worth it. On the way home, you couldn't stop talking about what a terrific show the band put on; you couldn't wait to tell the others kids about it. But the next day, hunched over a bowl of cereal, you read a review of the concert in the local paper. What? This guy slammed the sound system, thought the music was inane, and called the band a bunch of Backstreet wanna-bes! Who does he think he is?

Critics—they're everywhere. Even staring back at you in the mirror. The only real difference is that professional critics get paid to judge the way people perform, while amateur critics—everybody else—do it for free. You don't think you're critical? Some people are plagued by a critical spirit, and maybe you're not that bad. But if you're a living, breathing human, you do pass judgment on people and the things they do, and some of it is undoubtedly unfair. Even if you manage to zip your lips, your critical attitude is still there. But there's really good news for anyone (like you!) who wants to change his or her judgmental ways.

Like most negative traits, the tendency to criticize has a positive counterpart, and that's where the good news comes into play. A critical person often has great ideas for the best way to get things done. When you feel the urge to criticize the activities your youth group is planning or the way the decorations are turning out for your school's homecoming, all you have to do is resist the temptation, roll up your sleeves, and get to work. You have a much-needed contribution to make.

Whenever you find yourself criticizing individuals, however, a signal should go off in your head alerting you to the fact that this is a Golden Rule moment. That should stop your critical thoughts dead in their tracks. And remember this: To apply the Golden Rule as found in Matthew 7:12, you can't just avoid treating another person badly—you have to treat the person well, the way you'd like to be treated.

Most people know the Golden Rule, but few actually live by it. Be the first one on your block to follow it. Zip your lips, allow God to change your attitude, and turn your critical thoughts into an opportunity to do good to others.

I Will

Depend on God to help me change my negative
attitudes.   yes _____   no _____

Turn my criticisms into opportunities to do good.   yes _____   no _____

Practice living by the Golden Rule.   yes _____   no _____

Keep my critical thoughts to myself.   yes _____   no _____

Help out when I see people doing something that
could be done in a better way.   yes _____   no _____

Realize that although everyone judges other
people, I can control my critical thoughts.   yes _____   no _____

Things to Do

☐ Write out the Golden Rule and list the ways you can apply it to your
family members, your friends, and your teachers and church leaders.

☐ Ask God to help you conquer your judgmental nature.

☐ Meditate on Jesus' words in Matthew 7:1–12.

☐ List other positive counterparts to criticism, like discernment. Make a
commitment to developing those character traits.

☐ Volunteer to work on a project you've been critical of.

☐ Write a positive review of one of your church's projects.

Things to Remember

Jesus said, "Therefore, whatever you want men to do to you, do also to them, for this is the Law and the Prophets."

MATTHEW 7:12 NKJV

Jesus said, Judge not, and ye shall not be judged: condemn not, and ye shall not be condemned: forgive, and ye shall be forgiven.

LUKE 6:37 KJV

Let us not judge one another anymore, but rather resolve this, not to put a stumbling block or a cause to fall in our brother's way.

ROMANS 14:13 NKJV

Who are you to criticize God? Should the thing made say to the one who made it, "Why have you made me like this?"

ROMANS 9:20 TLB

Jesus said, "Why do you look at the speck in your brother's eyes, but do not consider the plank in your own eye? Or how can you say to your brother, 'Let me remove the speck from your eye'; and look, a plank is in your own eye? Hypocrite! First remove the plank from your own eye, and then you will see clearly to remove the speck from your brother's eye."

MATTHEW 7:3–5 NKJV

Any fool can criticize, condemn and complain—and most do.

DALE CARNEGIE

A Different Kind of Love

Jesus said, *"God so loved the world that He gave His only begotten Son, that whoever believes in Him should not perish but have everlasting life."*

—John 3:16 NKJV

Sacrifice reveals your love. Sacrifice. That's a loaded word—loaded, that is, with all kinds of images. And you never know what kind of images people are thinking of when they hear the word. Some people think of sacrifice as a waste: She sacrificed her career just to stay home with all those kids. Others think of it as some kind of loss: He sacrificed his teenage years trying to qualify for the Olympics, and he didn't make the cut. Still others think of dead animals, and there's no need to go there. But what about you? Do you think of sacrifice as a difficult obligation, something you have to give up for God? Or do you approach sacrifice with a joyful heart, thrilled that you have the opportunity to let go of something you value for the sake of a greater purpose?

That's really what sacrifice is, and God the Father gave us the ultimate example of sacrifice when He gave up something He valued—Jesus—for the sake of a greater purpose—your salvation from sin. The image of Jesus suffering on the cross is an indelible one for those who truly understand what His death means in their lives. It was the supreme example of a different kind of love, one that doesn't take but rather gives. It's a love that carries no hint of personal gain. And it's the kind of love God wants you to have for others.

You know your love is sacrificial when you can honestly say you are willing to lay down your life for someone else. But that's difficult for most people to relate to, because most people are never in a situation to sacrifice their lives for someone else. It may be more helpful to think of sacrificial love as a willingness to live for other people by serving them. It's the kind of love that joyfully gives up something of value—like time or money or even physical energy and labor—for the greater purpose of showing the depth of God's love.

What do you value that you are willing to give up for God? Are you willing to sacrifice your time to deliver bags of food to needy families, or your money—beyond your tithe— to support a special mission project, or your energy to pull weeds and mow the lawn for an elderly neighbor? As you sacrificially give, your actions reveal the God of love to those you serve.

I Will

Develop a heart of sacrificial service to others.   ___yes___ ___no___

Realize the magnitude of what God
sacrificed for me.   ___yes___ ___no___

Remember that sacrifice is not an option for one
who truly loves Jesus.   ___yes___ ___no___

Change my attitude from one of having to
sacrifice to one of getting to sacrifice.   ___yes___ ___no___

Define my love for others by my willingness to
give up things I value for their sake.   ___yes___ ___no___

Things to Do

☐ Thank God for sacrificing His Son so you could have eternal life.

☐ Think of what it means to offer up a "sacrifice of praise" to God,
then do it.

☐ Dedicate a sacrificial amount of time to prayer this week.

☐ Volunteer to do something at church that you would rather not do, at a
time you'd rather not do it.

☐ Offer to run errands, baby-sit, or help out a neighbor in some other
way—when it's convenient for the neighbor rather than for you.
Graciously refuse to accept anything in return.

Things to Remember

We love Him because He first loved us.

1 JOHN 4:19 NKJV

Paul wrote: I beseech you therefore, brethren, by the mercies of God, that you present your bodies a living sacrifice, holy, acceptable to God, which is your seasonable service.

ROMANS 12:1 NKJV

This is love: not that we loved God, but that he loved us and sent his Son as an atoning sacrifice for our sins.

1 JOHN 4:10 NIV

Through Jesus we should always bring God a sacrifice of praise, that is, words that acknowledge him. Don't forget to do good things for others and to share what you have with them. These are the kinds of sacrifices that please God.

HEBREWS 13:15–16 GOD'S WORD

Be imitators of God as dear children. And walk in love, as Christ also has loved us and given Himself for us, an offering and a sacrifice to God for a sweet-smelling aroma.

EPHESIANS 5:1–2 NKJV

· ·

The key to faith is what we are willing to sacrifice to obtain it.

ELDER CLOWARD

There's only one effectively redemptive sacrifice, the sacrifice of self-will to make room for the knowledge of God.

ALDOUS HUXLEY

You First

You younger people, submit yourselves to your elders. Yes, all of you be submissive to one another, and be clothed with humility, for "God resists the proud, but gives grace to the humble."

—1 Peter 5:5 NKJV

High above you, an agile young woman in a brightly colored costume appears to be the very definition of confidence. Never looking down, she places one foot before the other, sometimes quickly, sometimes slowly, and even takes an occasional hop—all on a path so narrow that you hold your breath until she safely makes it to the end. She's a tightrope walker whose circus act seldom fails to wow the crowd assembled below.

Learning to walk in humility is a bit like learning to keep your balance on a tightrope. On the one hand, you know you're not supposed to exalt yourself in any way. But a misstep in that direction threatens to turn you into a doormat for other people to trample on. On the other hand, you know that you're a child of the King, and you should never have to grovel before anyone. But a misstep in that direction turns you into a haughty, swaggering jerk. So how can you walk this tightrope without falling off?

Think of the tightrope as representing the truth about who you are. You are a complex individual with strengths and weaknesses. You have noble aspirations and selfish desires. You want to end world hunger and clobber the kid down the block. You pray for your friend to get saved and tell your little brother to get lost. In short, you're neither all good nor all bad. You're you.

Accepting the truth about yourself helps keep you humble. If you think more highly of yourself than you should, you're guilty of pride. If you think less of yourself than you should, you deny the handiwork of the One who created you. But once you have a firm handle on the truth about yourself—that you are a flawed human being who has been adopted into the eternal family of God—you'll be able to walk in the kind of humility that pleases the Father.

As that truth seeps into your spirit, your God-pleasing humility begins to express itself in practical ways. You develop a you-first mentality, one that places others ahead of yourself. You find yourself in the potluck line saying things like "No, no—you go first. Please." (What was that? you may think at first. Did I really let her get to the fried chicken before I did?) Or you give up your seat during a crowded (and no doubt long!) church service so that someone else may sit down. You leave the last doughnut in the box because you know it's your sister's favorite kind.

On a deeper level, your newfound sense of humility expresses itself in your relationship with God. Your spirit overflows with gratitude for all that He is and all that He has done for you. You learn not to run ahead of God, thinking that your way is somehow better than His. No, you develop a you-first mentality toward Him as well: "Lord, You go ahead and show me Your will. I will follow You." True humility makes you teachable, both by God and by other people that He has placed in your life for that purpose.

Jesus knew what He was doing when He used children to show the disciples the kind of humility He wanted them to have; suggesting that these rough-edged men become like children was likely to bring out the pride in them. You can imagine their thoughts: What? I'm a full-grown man, tough to the core. Why should I go back to behaving like a little kid? That's just what Jesus wanted them to see—that they were relying on their own strength rather than displaying a childlike trust in the Lord. And He wanted them to learn the truth about themselves—that they were handpicked to follow Him, but with that honor came the requirement that they humble themselves and submit their will to His.

That's His requirement for you as well. Learn to confidently walk that tightrope of truth by developing a humble spirit. As you practice humility by applying a you-first approach to the way to treat other people, you'll begin to feel better about yourself, and your relationships with others will be characterized by a greater sense of peace and unity. Most important, you'll be in right relationship with the Father.

I Will

Develop a childlike trust in God.

yes _____ no _____

Accept the truth about who I am.

yes _____ no _____

Think of others before myself.

yes _____ no _____

Be aware of the pride in my life and resolve to
overcome it.

yes _____ **no** _____

Realize that humbling myself does not mean I
have to grovel.

yes _____ no _____

Develop a teachable spirit.

yes _____ no _____

Things to Do

☐ Ask God to show you the areas of your life in which you need to be
more humble.

☐ Read about the Pharisee and the tax collector in Luke 18 for insight into
God's view of pride and humility.

☐ The Bible tells us to be clothed with humility. Meditate on what that
means and how you can accomplish it.

☐ Go through the day tomorrow with a you-first mentality and make note
of all the opportunities you have to let others go before you.

☐ List the practical ways you can display humility toward your parents
and the other significant people in your life.

Things to Remember

Jesus called a small child over to him and put the child among them. Then he said, "I assure you, unless you turn from your sins and become as little children, you will never get into the Kingdom of Heaven. Therefore, anyone who becomes as humble as this little child is the greatest in the Kingdom of Heaven."

MATTHEW 18:2–4 NLT

Let nothing be done through selfish ambition or conceit, but in lowliness of mind let each esteem others better than himself.

—PHILIPPIANS 2:3 NKJV

By humility and the fear of the LORD are riches and honor and life.

PROVERBS 22:4 NKJV

Jesus said, "Whoever exalts himself will be humbled, and he who humbles himself will be exalted."

LUKE 14:11 NKJV

Surely He scorns the scornful, but gives grace to the humble.

PROVERBS 3:34 NKJV

You will save the humble people, but will bring down haughty looks.

PSALM 18:27 NKJV

When pride comes, then comes disgrace; but wisdom is with the humble.

PROVERBS 11:2 NRSV

I have made all these things. "That is why all these things have come into being," declares the LORD. I will pay attention to those who are humble and sorry [for their sins] and who tremble at my word.

ISAIAH 66:2 GOD'S WORD

A servant of the Lord must not quarrel but be gentle to all, able to teach, patient, in humility correcting those who are in opposition, if God perhaps will grant them repentance, so that they may know the truth.

2 TIMOTHY 2:24–25 NKJV

The humble He guides in justice, and the humble He teaches His way.

PSALM 25:9 NKJV

It is good for the young to submit to the yoke of [the LORD's] discipline.

LAMENTATIONS 3:27 NLT

It is no great thing to be humble when you are brought low; but to be humble when you are praised is a great and rare attainment.

—SAINT BERNARD OF CLAIRVAUX

Nothing sets a person so much out of the devil's reach as humility.

—JONATHAN EDWARDS

Whatever Works

Two are better than one, because they have a good reward for their labor.

—*Ecclesiastes 4:9* NKJV

Just your kind of luck—you've been assigned to work on a history project with three space cadets. These kids are so far out there that they wouldn't know solid ground if they fell on it. Getting them to work on the project in any kind of logical way is going to be like trying to rope a cloud and rein it in.

You know, absolutely know, that the best way to start this project is with a clear and concise timeline. But no. The others think focusing on names and dates and events is a waste of time; philosophical ideas and abstract concepts are what matter. You argue, you plead, you cajole. They don't seem to hear you; they're off on their own orbital path, discussing theories and who knows what else among themselves.

This would be a good time for you to back off. Decide that whatever the group decides, you'll go along with it.

The project is hardly a matter of life-and-death, and no one is asking you to violate your conscience or some biblical precept. Your ability to let go of your own agenda and cooperate with the others will contribute immeasurably to the success of the project.

Cooperation with others makes the work go better. Even if your way of doing things seems better, when you cooperate with others the work goes more smoothly. The "inferior" way actually becomes the better way, because instead of wasting time trying to bring others around to your point of view, you're helping the group get the work done.

The apostle Paul continually hammered home the importance of believers working together in harmony. Disputes within the early church distracted Christians from the work of spreading the gospel and didn't exactly attract outsiders to the fold. Even today, Christians argue over insignificant details, and the world looks on in disgust. Each time you experience this kind of situation with other believers, you're doing your part, however small it may seem, to encourage a cooperative spirit within the church.

But when should most of these moments occur? In the presence of God. Nothing delights the heart of God more than to hear one of His followers say, "I'll cooperate with You in whatever You ask of me." Let Him hear you say those words—and be prepared to cooperate with His Spirit as He leads you into His will.

I Will

Cooperate with God as He reveals His will to me.   *yes*   *no*

Realize that others will not always be willing to do things my way.   *yes*   *no*

Do what I can to encourage a cooperative spirit within the church.   *yes*   *no*

Know to let go of my own agenda when it starts to get in the way of my relationships.   *yes*   *no*

Work in harmony with others to get the job done.   *yes*   *no*

Place unity with other believers above my own wishes.   *yes*   *no*

Things to Do

☐ Ask God to help you develop a cooperative spirit.

☐ Read Acts 2:40–47 to see the connection between cooperation among believers and the impact on the unbelieving world around them.

☐ Read 1 Corinthians 1:10–17, Paul's disapproval of division in the church.

☐ Identify one activity you're involved in right now in which you could be more cooperative.

☐ List some practical ways you can contribute to unity within your youth group or your circle of Christian friends.

Things to Remember

Speaking the truth in love, we will in all things grow up into him who is the Head, that is, Christ. From him the whole body, joined and held together by every supporting ligament, grows and builds itself up in love, as each part does its work.

EPHESIANS 4:15–16 NIV

Shecaniah said to Ezra, "Take courage, for it is your duty to tell us how to proceed in setting things straight, and we will cooperate fully."

EZRA 10:4 NLT

The multitude of those who believed were of one heart and one soul; neither did anyone say that any of the things he possessed was his own, but they had all things in common.

ACTS 4:32 NKJV

All of you should agree and have concern and love for each other. You should also be kind and humble.

1 PETER 3:8 CEV

· ·

Always try to do something for the other fellow and you will be agreeably surprised how things come your way— how many pleasing things are done for you.

CLAUDE M. BRISTOL

The obedience of Jesus is not simply submission but real striving, cooperation, activity.

JOHN J. VINCENT

COMPLAINING

Complaint Department

Do all things without complaining and disputing.
—Philippians 2:14 NKJV

Have you ever heard a professional baseball player grouse about his salary? The guy—and he could be any number of players, it seems—probably makes several million a year, and there he is, griping to the TV cameras and anyone who'll listen that he's underpaid. *What's he got to complain about?* you think. *He's got it made. He's got everything he needs! What a* _____ [fill in the blank].

Hold on there. Before you start calling this multimillionaire all kinds of not-so-godly names, back off, count to ten, and take an inventory of some of the things you've said and thought over the past, oh, week or so. Think you could find a complaint or two in your memory bank? Most likely you can, because it's a rare person who never complains. You may even need to go on a "complaint fast." That's just like the kind of fast you read about in the Bible, only you don't give up food. You give up complaining.

So what does a complaint fast mean in real life? It means that you don't whine when your mom asks you to help her in the kitchen. You don't grumble when your dad reminds you to take out the trash. You don't moan when you find out you have to do a project for the science fair (well... just don't moan out loud, all right?). You don't roll your eyes when your kid sister asks you to help her create a snug little hideout in her room. (Oh, you didn't realize that you can complain without even opening your mouth? Well, you can—and you probably do!)

Imagine yourself in all those scenarios—actually picture yourself whining to your mother, grumbling to your father, moaning to your teacher, rolling your eyes at your sister. Not a pretty series of snapshots, is it? That's because complaining is downright unattractive. It won't win you any beauty pageants, and it won't win you any popularity contests, either. And you can forget all about winning the coveted good citizenship award this year!

So—do you think you're ready to try a complaint fast? You can start by praying, and you can start your prayer by asking God to forgive you for complaining so much. Then ask Him to guide you and strengthen you as you try to give up this obnoxious habit for a certain amount of time—several days, maybe a week, whatever commitment He leads you to make. During that time, you can count on God to take a poke at your conscience each time you complain or are tempted to complain. Your immediate repentance when you realize you've complained, and your immediate obedience when you realize you're about to complain, will determine the success of your fast.

When it's all over, you'll likely be so sick of dealing with your own complaining spirit that you'll do your best to avoid grumbling in the future. Concentrating to that extent on the habit of complaining makes you more aware than ever of how frequently you lapse into certain wrong habits. And it ought to make you stop and think about the other fasts you need to go on: jealousy fast, criticism fast, gossip fast, dishonesty fast...the list could get pretty long! This would be a good time to thank God for whatever success you've had on your fast—and for all that you already have victory over.

When it comes right down to it, complaining is a pretty lousy way to repay God for all that He's done for you. He's given you more than you could have ever hoped to have in this life had you never met Him, starting with His eternal and unconditional love. When you factor in all that He is and all that He has—and His willingness and desire to share it all with you—well, just try to find a legitimate reason to moan and groan in light of all that!

The next time you're tempted to complain, think about that multimillionaire baseball player. Only now, apply the thoughts you had toward him to yourself: What have I got to complain about? I've got it made! I've got everything I need! What a blessed person I am!

I Will

Understand that it's an affront to God to grumble
about my life.

    yes   *no*

Appreciate all the blessings God has
provided for me.

    yes   *no*

Realize that complaining is not just a string of
words but also an attitude of the heart.

    yes   *no*

Stop complaining.

    yes   *no*

Expect God's Spirit to alert me to those situations
that I'm tempted to complain about.

    yes   *no*

Things to Do

☐ Read how God dealt with the complaints of the Israelites in Exodus 16
and Numbers 14 to get a glimpse of how He feels about those who
complain.

☐ Ask the Lord to replace your complaining spirit with
a spirit of gratitude.

☐ Go on a complaint fast.

☐ Think back to the things you've complained about in the past week.
When you've stopped laughing at your foolishness, ask God
to forgive you.

☐ Do a job around the house that you've complained about in the past.
Have a camera ready to capture your parents' shocked expressions.

Things to Remember

These are grumblers, complainers, walking according to their own lusts; and they mouth great swelling words, flattering people to gain advantage.

JUDE 1:16 NKJV

Nor [let us] complain, as some of them also complained, and were destroyed by the destroyer.

1 CORINTHIANS 10:10 NKJV

Do not grumble against one another, brethren, lest you be condemned. Behold, the Judge is standing at the door!

—JAMES 5:9 NKJV

Martha was the jittery type, and she was worrying over the big dinner she was preparing. She came to Jesus and said, "Sir, doesn't it seem unfair to you that my sister just sits here while I do all the work? Tell her to come and help me."

LUKE 10:40 TLB

The LORD said, "How long shall I bear with this evil congregation who complain against Me? I have heard the complaints which the children of Israel make against Me."

NUMBERS 14:27 NKJV

Why should we, mere humans, complain
when we are punished for our sins?

LAMENTATIONS 3:39 NLT

The Ephraimites spoke against God, saying,
"Can God spread a table in the wilderness?
Even though he struck the rock so that water
gushed out and torrents overflowed, can he
also give bread, or provide meat for his
people?"

PSALM 78:19–20 NRSV

People's own foolishness ruins their lives,
but in their minds they blame the LORD.

PROVERBS 19:3 NCV

Moses said, "This shall be seen when the
LORD gives you meat to eat in the evening,
and in the morning bread to the full; for the
LORD hears your complaints which you
make against Him. And what are we? Your
complaints are not against us but against
the LORD."

EXODUS 16:8 NKJV

The Jews then complained about Him,
because He said, "I am the bread which
came down from heaven." And they said, "Is
not this Jesus, the son of Joseph, whose
father and mother we know? How is it then
that He says, 'I have come down from
heaven'?" Jesus therefore answered and said
to them, "Do not murmur among
yourselves."

JOHN 6:41–43 NKJV

Complain as
little as possible
of your wrongs,
for, as a general
rule, you may be
sure that
complaining is
sin: because
self-love always
magnifies our
injuries.

—SAINT FRANCIS DE
SALES

There are two
kinds of
discontent in
this world. The
discontent that
works, and the
discontent that
wrings its hands.
The first gets
what it wants.
The second loses
what it has.

—GORDON GRAHAM

24/7

Walk circumspectly, not as fools but as wise, redeeming the time, because the days are evil.
—Ephesians 5:15–16 NKJV

You're dog-tired, and you just want to drift off into a deep sleep. Just as you start to nod off, a nagging thought jars you: You didn't spend any time with God today. Oh well, you think. He'll forgive me. You know that's a feeble attempt at quieting your conscience, so you try a seemingly foolproof approach: I just didn't have time today. Nobody has time anymore, right?

Ah, that's where you're wrong, you and lots of other people. Most people have about forty-four hours of free time each week—and students who don't work have more than that. So where does it all go? And why don't you have time for God?

Life is filled with potential time-wasters: television, the Internet, phone calls, and the like. But lots of time is also wasted by lack of planning and organization, indecision, daydreaming, and misplaced priorities. Even a lack of understanding can cause you to waste time: You play a computer game to unwind after school, when the best "unwinder" is time spent in the presence of God. Time-wasters rob you of those forty-four hours and derail your spiritual growth in the process.

In one sense, everyone has the same amount of time, twenty-four hours each day. But in another sense, everyone has a different amount of time, their life span—and even people who have lived a long time talk about how short life seems to be. God is well aware of that, and in His word He often admonished people to make the most of their time on earth. (By "making the most of their time," He meant seeking Him and His ways, not partying 24/7!)

You can make the most of your time by actually scheduling time with God each day. Without that kind of planning—in essence, making an appointment with God—the opportunity is likely to slip away. Some people tithe their time, intentionally spending a tenth of it pursuing the things of God. A time tithe translates into 2.4 hours a day! Pretty daunting, isn't it? If you're not ready for that, start by committing a realistic amount of time to God each day. Make it a priority, and keep your commitment. (You wouldn't stand up a date, would you? God is more important than any date you'll ever have; don't even think of standing Him up!) Then when you lay your head on your pillow each night, you can lay aside your feeble excuses as well.

I Will

Commit a realistic amount of time to God
each day.   _yes_   _no_

Learn to unwind in the presence of God.   _yes_   _no_

Place a high priority on prayer, Bible study, and
my relationship with God.   _yes_   _no_

Be aware of the time-wasters in my life.   _yes_   _no_

Realize that I have more spare time than I
think I do.   _yes_   _no_

Make the most of whatever time I have left
on earth.   _yes_   _no_

Things to Do

☐ Ask God to be the Lord of your time.

☐ Memorize Ecclesiastes 12:1.

☐ Find a time management system that you will actually use, and
customize it for your unique needs.

☐ Make a list of your personal time-wasters. Eliminate one completely
and figure out how to cut down on the rest.

☐ Create a schedule for the coming week, starting only with obligations
(school, work) and important activities (church, Bible study). Add the
unimportant stuff you'd like to do only after you've scheduled the
important things.

Things to Remember

Mordecai told them to answer Esther… "If you remain completely silent at this time, relief and deliverance will arise for the Jews from another place, but you and your father's house will perish. Yet who knows whether you have come to the kingdom for such a time as this?"

ESTHER 4:13–14 NKJV

He who keeps his command will experience nothing harmful; and a wise man's heart discerns both time and judgment.

ECCLESIASTES 8:5 NKJV

Ezra said, "Go, eat rich foods, drink sweet drinks, and send portions to those who cannot provide for themselves. Today is a holy day for the LORD. Don't be sad because the joy you have in the Lord is your strength."

NEHEMIAH 8:10 GOD'S WORD

To everything there is a season, a time for every purpose under heaven.

ECCLESIASTES 3:1 NKJV

• •

There is a time to be born, and a time to die, says Solomon, and it is the memento of a truly wise man. But there is an interval between these two times of infinite importance.

LEGH RICHMOND

God created time and gave it to us. It is his fundamental gift, for all other gifts are conditioned upon it. Why should we give it so grudgingly to his service?

E. A. ROUNTREE

Just Do It

*All these blessings shall come upon you and overtake you,
because you obey the voice of the Lord your God.*
—*Deuteronomy 28:2* NKJV

Jon's boss—Mr. Mac Donald—thought Jon was a model employee at Mac's burger franchise. Jon seemed to do his job with relish. But when Big Mac wasn't around, which was often, Jon slacked off, bullying the rest of his crew—mostly younger high-school students—with disturbing threats. His unsuspecting boss promoted him to franchise manager.

Across the street, Cynthia worked after school at a pet store owned by a man who was messier and smellier than the living inventory. She swore that the next time he barked at her to clean the puppies' cages, she was going to bark right back. But when the next time came, who was in the store but Dustin Timberline, the coolest guy in town. Instead of barking, Cynthia smiled sweetly as she glanced at Dustin on her way to scoop out the—um, stuff—from the cages.

A mile away, Kerry swept the floor of the beauty shop for the nth time. "Go clean the restroom!" the manager ordered. It's

OK, she thought, brushing off Janet's clipped manner. She's stressed over the lack of business. Cleaning the restroom will give me a chance to pray for her in private.

Three obedient employees, right? They all did what they were told to do; technically they all obeyed. But only Kerry met God's definition of genuine obedience—a submissive attitude of the heart coupled with immediate action.

Can you see the differences in the way Jon, Cynthia, and Kerry complied with the demands of their jobs? Jon's obedience was limited and was motivated by selfishness; Cynthia's obedience was motivated by Dustin's presence—she was afraid of looking bad in front of him. But Kerry's obedience was motivated by love—if not for Janet, then for her ultimate boss, God Himself.

Genuine love is the key to genuine obedience. If you love God, you will obey Him. If you love God, you will also follow His command to obey your parents and anyone else in authority over you. But remember: His brand of obedience requires a major heart adjustment; no more obeying on the outside while rebelling on the inside.

Your unquestioned obedience to the will of God will bring you a measure of joy and peace that you simply can't experience when you're living in disobedience. The earlier you learn that, the better. Just wait a while and ask Jon and Cynthia—because eventually, a disobedient spirit can't help but show its ugly face to the world.

I Will

Understand that ultimately, God is my boss.   _yes_   _no_

Have an attitude of immediate obedience to those
in authority over me.   _yes_   _no_

Be thankful for the authority figures that God has
placed in my life to protect and instruct me.   _yes_   _no_

Make sure my obedience is motivated by love.   _yes_   _no_

Expect my obedience to produce joy and peace.   _yes_   _no_

Decide to take advantage of unpleasant tasks by
praying through them.   _yes_   _no_

Things to Do

☐ Repent of your disobedience toward God and others, and accept His
forgiveness.

☐ Ask God to change your heart and give you an obedient spirit.

☐ Read through one of the Gospels to learn from Jesus' example of
obedience to the Father.

☐ Memorize Matthew 7:21.

☐ Pray for those in authority over you.

☐ Discover what motivates your obedience by paying close attention to
the way you react to authority figures for the next few days. Make sure
at least one day is a school day or a work day.

Things to Remember

Whoever resists the authority resists the ordinance of God, and those who resist will bring judgment on themselves.

ROMANS 13:2 NKJV

Solomon wrote: My father also taught me, and said to me: "Let your heart retain my words; keep my commands, and live."

PROVERBS 4:4 NKJV

Jesus said, "Not everyone who says to Me, 'Lord, Lord,' will enter the kingdom of heaven, but he who does the will of My Father who is in heaven."

MATTHEW 7:21 NASB

The time has come for judgment to begin at the house of God; and if it begins with us first, what will be the end of those who do not obey the gospel of God?

1 PETER 4:17 NKJV

Through Christ, God gave me the special work of an apostle, which was to lead people of all nations to believe and obey. I do this work for him.

ROMANS 1:5 NCV

Obedience to God is the most infallible evidence of sincere and supreme love to him.

NATHANAEL EMMONS

I find the doing of the will of God leaves me no time for disputing about His plans.

GEORGE MACDONALD

Soul Survivor

God is our refuge and strength, a very present help in trouble.

—Psalm 46:1 NKJV

So here you are, a Scripture-promise-card-carrying member of the family of God, and you figure your life ought to be pretty close to perfect. At least that's what some of your Christian friends implied before you came to know God. "Ask Jesus into your heart, and all your troubles will go away." Isn't that what they said? you think, mentally listing the ordeals you've faced since that day. Hopefully, that's not what they actually said. Maybe that's just what you heard—or maybe your friends hadn't read as far as the book of James. Because James, God bless him, laid it on the line right after he said hello: You will encounter trials. This life you've gotten yourself into is definitely not for the weak or timid or fearful.

James also made no bones about how you should react to trials: You're supposed to rejoice! That sounds crazy until you read on and find out why. Your trials, it seems, are tailor-made to produce patience, and that's a sure sign of maturity. So all these trials are there to help you grow spiritually—depending, of course, on how you respond to them. You can't expect your trials to turn into faith-filled triumphs if you walk around in a self-pitying funk all day. The triumph comes as soon as you turn to God and count on Him to see you through.

Your friends, by the way, also should have read the book that follows James, one of two written by the apostle Peter, who knew something about enduring trials. He even told you to expect fiery trials and was amazed by those believers who thought it was weird that they had to go through these things. It's as if he was asking, "What's the matter with you? Didn't you know your faith would need to be tested by fire? How else can your faith become more precious than gold itself?" You will survive God's refining fire, and you will come out stronger as a result.

The next time you encounter a trial—an illness, an accident, a major disappointment—turn to God immediately and thank Him, not for the trial itself but for the purifying work He's doing in your life. When you share the gospel with others, you can leave out the fiery trials bit, but just don't go promising a trouble-free life either. Keep the words of your two new friends—James and Peter, that is—firmly planted in your mind.

I Will

Remember to turn to God immediately when trials
come my way.

yes   *no*

Expect my faith to be tested.

yes   *no*

Be thankful and joyful that my faith is being tested
as I endure the trials in my life.

yes   *no*

Be careful not to promise a carefree life when I
share the gospel with others.

yes   *no*

Understand that having patience during difficult
times is a sign of maturity.

yes   *no*

Things to Do

- [ ] Read the first chapter of James, paying attention to the close connection between trials, patience, maturity, and wisdom.

- [ ] Thank God for the beneficial results of the trials you've endured, even if you can't see the blessings yet.

- [ ] Practice sharing the gospel in a truthful way, being careful to avoid unscriptural promises and overstatements.

- [ ] Meditate on the concept of God being a "refuge, a very present help in trouble."

- [ ] List the ways a joyful attitude could have an impact on your response to a specific trial—say, a hypothetical car crash or something you're actually going through right now.

Things to Remember

The LORD said, "Fear not, for I am with you; Be not dismayed, for I am your God. I will strengthen you, Yes, I will help you, I will uphold you with My righteous right hand."

ISAIAH 41:10 NKJV

If you faint in the day of adversity, your strength is small.

PROVERBS 24:10 NKJV

Consider it all joy, my brethren, when you encounter various trials.

JAMES 1:2 NASB

Be truly glad! There is wonderful joy ahead, even though the going is rough for a while down here. These trials are only to test your faith, to see whether or not it is strong and pure.

1 PETER 1:6–7 TLB

Whoever listens to [Wisdom] will dwell safely, and will be secure, without fear of evil.

PROVERBS 1:33 NKJV

· ·

The only way to learn strong faith is to endure great trials. I have learned my faith by standing firm amid severe testings.

GEORGE MÜLLER

The chief pang of most trials is not so much the actual suffering itself as our own spirit of resistance to it.

JEAN NICHOLAS GROU

Ever After

Keep your heart with all diligence, for out of it spring the
issues of life.

—*Proverbs 4:23 NKJV*

This is finally it—you've met the one! He's popular, he's
handsome, he takes you nice places and makes your heart
flutter; she's beautiful and sweet and irresistible, and she has
this great laugh. And you both love the Lord! What could be
better?

Plenty, starting with a couple of no-brainers, like having
God's seal of approval on your relationship and basing your
attraction on something other than superficial traits. If you
want a love that's going to last "ever after," you need to
understand a few things.

Romantic love is without a doubt one of the coolest of
God's gifts. It brings out the best in you if you handle it
carefully. It makes all your senses come alive, almost to the
point of overload. Like all of God's gifts, however, this one
can be abused. When it is, it leaves devastated lives in its
wake. So before you take the plunge into a love-drenched
relationship, back off the edge and pay attention to what God

has to say about this awesome gift.

Start with His repeated admonitions, first to the Israelites and then to the early church, to avoid becoming entangled with anyone outside the family of faith. Maybe your intended has memorized hundreds of Bible verses and never misses a youth group meeting. To put it bluntly, that doesn't mean a thing. What do you know of her private relationship with God? What are his spiritual hopes and dreams for the future? How do you relate to God as a couple?

The answers to those and other questions are critical, because marriage is the hardest blessing you'll ever have (until the kids come, but that's another story altogether). Marriage? Where did that come from? You're just talking about being in love! But if you're not ready to think seriously about marriage, you're not ready to fall in love. Why not? Because if the relationship isn't leading toward marriage, you're just toying with another person's heart. You're in love with the idea of being in love, and the shine wears off of that really fast.

Before you go checking out potential mates, take a look at some of the qualities God suggests you look for; they may surprise you. Did you know that young women are encouraged to seek a man who treats animals well, has compassion for the poor, and makes sound business decisions? Those qualities probably aren't on your Ideal Husband list. And guys—when you go pursuing a wife, place a low priority on her beauty, make sure she fears the Lord, and run in the opposite direction if she's argumentative! These and other characteristics of a suitable mate are all found in the book of Proverbs—a great place to spend a lot of time if you're thinking about marriage.

After you've done all that, you still need to trust God completely in this area of your life. That's difficult when your heart is doing somersaults; you're afraid that if you let this one go, there's no telling what God's going to come up with. You love Him and all, but you worry that He might be a bit lacking in the taste department. But who knows what you need better than God does? Who better understands what you desire in a mate? Who wants you to have a successful marriage more than God does? He won't hook you up with someone you can't stand to look at for an evening, let alone the rest of your life. Remember, He loves you—and torture is not an aspect of love.

Avoid serious relationships until you're ready for marriage; meanwhile, socialize in a crowd or with different groups of friends. Don't confuse physical attraction with love; get a clear idea of the inner qualities you want in a mate and don't compromise on them. Never, ever expect the person to change. What you see is what you're going to get, not some improved version you hope to create. Hold out for that one who cherishes you, treats you like gold, and allows you to be yourself. Focus on being the right person instead of finding the right person. Most of all, trust God to give you wisdom and discernment and peace of mind about your decision.

I Will

Trust God's timing when it comes to getting involved in a serious relationship.

yes _____ no _____

Hold out for God's best when it comes to love and marriage.

yes _____ no _____

Learn to rely more on a person's inner qualities than on his or her outward appearance.

yes _____ no _____

Limit the field of potential mates to those on the same spiritual wavelength I'm on.

yes _____ no _____

Focus on being the right person for the one I will eventually marry.

yes _____ no _____

Things to Do

☐ Ask God to work in the life of your future mate, even though you may not know who that is and marriage could be a decade or more away.

☐ Ask God to use this time in your life to prepare you to be the right kind of mate.

☐ Make a list of all the characteristics you want in a mate. Pray over it, refine it according to God's leading, and entrust it to His care until the time is right.

☐ Now go through the book of Proverbs and write down the desirable characteristics of a husband and a wife. Compare them with those on your ideal-mate list and your own character.

Things to Remember

Do not be unequally yoked together with unbelievers. For what fellowship has righteousness with lawlessness? And what communion has light with darkness?

2 CORINTHIANS 6:14 NKJV

Those who live following their sinful selves think only about things that their sinful selves want. But those who live following the Spirit are thinking about the things the Spirit wants them to do.

ROMANS 8:5 NCV

Houses and riches are an inheritance from fathers, but a prudent wife is from the LORD.

—PROVERBS 19:14 NKJV

Charm is deceitful and beauty is passing, but a woman who fears the LORD, she shall be praised.

PROVERBS 31:30 NKJV

The Shulamite said: Let him kiss me with the kisses of his mouth—for your love is better than wine.

SONG OF SOLOMON 1:2 NKJV

Jacob served seven years for Rachel, and they seemed only a few days to him because of the love he had for her.

GENESIS 29:20 NKJV

A time to love, and a time to hate; a time of war, and a time of peace

ECCLESIASTES 3:8 NKJV

Young women of Jerusalem, swear to me by the gazelles or by the does in the field, that you will not awaken love or arouse love before its proper time.

SONG OF SOLOMON 3:5 GOD'S WORD

Love never stops being patient, never stops believing, never stops hoping, never gives up.

1 CORINTHIANS 13:7 GOD'S WORD

Love is strong as death, passion fierce as the grave. Its flashes are flashes of fire, a raging flame.

SONG OF SOLOMON 8:6 NRSV

Unfailing love and truth have met together. Righteousness and peace have kissed!

PSALM 85:10 NLT

Two souls with but a single thought, Two hearts that beat as one.

—FRANZ JOSEPH VON MÜNCH-BELLINGHAUSEN

Whoso loves believes the impossible.

—ELIZABETH BARRETT BROWNING

Power Up

Confess your trespasses to one another, and pray for one another, that you may be healed. The effective, fervent prayer of a righteous man avails much.

—James 5:16 NKJV

Suddenly, your palms are sweaty, your mind's a blank, your mouth won't move, and you can't find your voice. No, you haven't just seen the most beautiful creature on God's green earth—you've just been asked to say the closing prayer at your youth group meeting. Or how about this: You're the only one in the house. No one's expected home for hours. You kneel on the floor, figuring that now you'll be able to pray. But as the words come out, you feel self-conscious. You wonder if anyone is listening—including God!

If that's you, take heart. Lots of Christians talk a big talk about the importance of prayer, but few admit (or seem to remember) how difficult it can be, especially when you haven't had a whole lot of practice. You need some pointers to get you started, and there's no better place to start than the Bible.

Take a look at the Lord's Prayer. You're not expected to use those exact words, though there's nothing wrong with that. Jesus gave you His prayer as a model for your own: acknowledging who God is, desiring His will to be accomplished on earth, asking for basic needs, seeking forgiveness and deliverance, and praising Him. You can't go wrong praying along those lines. As long as you avoid making it personal, this is a good way to pray in public.

You can also try praying the psalms. Many individual psalms were written as prayers to the Lord. Find those that express what's in your heart and pray them back to God. Since some psalms are intensely personal, save this for your private times of prayer. Find other scriptures you can pray back to God. "Lord, You say in Your word that where two or three are gathered, You are in their midst, so we believe You are with us now." Or, "Lord, according to Your word, if I confess my sins, You will be faithful to forgive me and lead me into righteousness." Depending on the scripture you choose, you can use this method for both public and private prayer.

There's nothing wrong with practicing in private until you're comfortable with public prayer. But never forget this: God is longing to hear you express to Him what's in your heart. Your eloquence is meaningless. What counts is the genuine love and faith behind your words, no matter how simple they may be.

I Will

Trust God to help me overcome my discomfort
with prayer, both public and private.   yes   no

Give God my fear when I pray publicly and my
self-consciousness when I pray privately.   yes   no

Realize that prayer is simply a matter of talking
with God.   yes   no

Pray in my own way, avoiding pompous,
eloquent—sounding words that I don't
normally use.   yes   no

Understand that the more I pray, the easier
it will get.   yes   no

Things to Do

☐ Study the Lord's Prayer and use it as a model to create your own
personal variation.

☐ Find a dozen psalms that you can memorize over time and pray back to
God.

☐ Create a special notebook to keep with your Bible for copying verses
that you can later pray back to God.

☐ Write down what you'd like to say to God in prayer. (There—you've
just prayed!)

☐ Read Fuel: Igniting Your Life with Passionate Prayer.

Things to Remember

Be anxious for nothing, but in everything by prayer and supplication, with thanksgiving, let your requests be made known to God.

PHILIPPIANS 4:6 NKJV

The LORD said, "It shall come to pass that before they call, I will answer; and while they are still speaking, I will hear."

ISAIAH 65:24 NKJV

Jesus said, If ye shall ask any thing in my name,
I will do it.

JOHN 14:14 KJV

Jesus said, "Whatever things you ask when you pray, believe that you receive them, and you will have them."

MARK 11:24 NKJV

The Lord said, "If My people who are called by My name will humble themselves, and pray and seek My face, and turn from their wicked ways, then I will hear from heaven, and will forgive their sin and heal their land."

2 CHRONICLES 7:14 NKJV

· ·

Prayer is not overcoming God's reluctance; it is laying hold of His highest willingness.

RICHARD CHENEVIX TRENCH

Let prayer be the key of the day and the bolt of the night.

JEAN PAUL RICHTER

Making the Cut

> To give prudence to the simple, to the young man knowledge and discretion.
>
> —Proverbs 1:4 NKJV

Grades—doesn't it seem as if your life revolves around them? If you're planning to go to college, your high school records are reduced to initialisms like GPA and SAT whose numbers determine which college will admit you and which scholarships you qualify for. Or if you're an "average" student—whatever that means—people don't expect much from you, forgetting that some of the most successful people in the world got straight C's all through high school and never even went to college.

If grades are the standard by which you gauge your potential to succeed, you're in trouble! Generally, your academic years are the only ones in which your grades will count for anything. Once you get out into the work world, no one will care how many times you made the honor roll or whether you failed geometry—unless, of course, you've been hired as an engineer, architect, math teacher, or the like. Does that mean you shouldn't strive to get good grades? No. You should always do your best and attempt to excel in whatever you do.

What will count in the years to come and in your future career are your character—who you are on the inside—and your ability to apply what you've learned in school to your life and to your work. You may think that the first will determine how well you succeed as a person and the second will determine how well you succeed in your career. But you'd be mistaken. Your character determines both kinds of success.

You can set unrealistic standards for the kind of grades you'd like to get, but you can never set your moral, ethical, and spiritual standards too high. You may be a solid D student when it comes to math but a straight A student when it comes to loving God and treating others with compassion and fairness and placing a high value on integrity. Which set of grades will matter for eternity?

If your parents are pressuring you to get better grades, you need to do your best to meet their expectations by working hard and relying on God to help you. If you're putting excessive, impossible pressure on yourself, stop. Making the academic cut is not worth it—making the eternal cut is. If you're going to put pressure on yourself, be sure it counts for something worthwhile—like living right while you're on earth and spending eternity with God.

I Will

Trust God to help me excel in whatever I do.

yes _no_

Stop thinking of grades as predictors of my chances
for success in the future.

yes _no_

Realize that my character will help determine how
well I succeed in my career.

yes _no_

Focus on developing high moral, ethical, and
spiritual standards.

yes _no_

Let up the pressure on myself to meet unrealistic
academic demands.

yes _no_

Things to Do

☐ Ask God to show you which character traits you need to improve and
thank Him in advance for the help He'll give you in making those
improvements.

☐ Ask God for the strength and power to adhere to the standards you've
set for your life.

☐ Read through one of the Gospels and write down everything you learn
about Christ's character.

☐ List the ways you can apply what you've learned about Jesus to your
own character standard.

☐ Rate your spiritual life by giving yourself grades in subjects like time
alone with God, Bible reading and study, prayer, obedience, and so
forth. See where there's room for improvement.

Things to Remember

"Who has known the mind of the Lord that he may instruct Him?" But we have the mind of Christ.

1 CORINTHIANS 2:16 NKJV

The soul of a lazy man desires, and has nothing; but the soul of the diligent shall be made rich.

PROVERBS 13:4 NKJV

Be diligent to present yourself approved to God, a worker who does not need to be ashamed, rightly dividing the word of truth.

2 TIMOTHY 2:15 NKJV

Be doers of the word, and not hearers only, deceiving yourselves.

JAMES 1:22 NKJV

Jesus said, "I can guarantee that unless you live a life that has God's approval and do it more faithfully than the scribes and Pharisees, you will never enter the kingdom of heaven."

MATTHEW 5:20 GOD'S WORD

For us, with the rule of right and wrong given us by Christ, there is nothing for which we have no standard.

LEO TOLSTOY

Ah, but a man's reach should exceed his grasp,
Or what's a heaven for?

ROBERT BROWNING

Instant Replay

He will not dwell unduly on the days of his life, because God keeps him busy with the joy of his heart.

—Ecclesiastes 5:20 NKJV

Notice the faraway look that some adults get when they're talking to you about your life. You're having a seemingly normal conversation with your uncle about your plans to go to college, and suddenly he looks off into the distance, nodding his head at the right moments but clearly not really with you anymore. Or you're telling your cousin about this guy you've been dating and how you figure you'll get married right after high school—and you realize your aunt is just within hearing distance, looking at you with a hint of sadness in her eyes. Your aunt and uncle are probably mentally replaying something in their past that they'd rather forget.

What you see in their eyes is regret—a deep and profound sorrow for the poor decisions in their past. Your uncle regrets not going to college; your aunt regrets getting married too soon. When they say they wish they could be seventeen again, it's not because they had such a great time as teenagers. It's because they'd like to have the opportunity to make better decisions, especially the ones that would affect the course of their lives for decades to come.

Living with regret creates an indescribably sad existence. As a teenager, you are in an incomparable position to make the right decisions in life, since most of the major decisions you'll have to make are still ahead of you. As a Christian, you're in the best position of all, because you have access to God's wisdom and the peace of mind He gives when you've made the right decision. Commit your future, with its myriad life-altering decisions, to God, and you'll never have to learn to live with regret.

Maybe, though, you've already made some serious mistakes that you wish you hadn't. While you can't go back and change the situation or its consequences, you can pick yourself up, brush yourself off, and get on with your life. But before you do, you'd be wise to spend a little time in the book of Acts with the apostle Paul.

If anyone had a good reason to regret the things he'd done in his life, it was Paul. He was an accomplice in the murder of Stephen, the first Christian martyr—if not as a stone-thrower, then at least as a cheering spectator. He persecuted Christians at every turn and was proud of it. Imagine how he must have felt when the Lord brought him to his knees and showed him how very wrong he was. But Paul had the good sense not only to fully accept Jesus' free gift of complete and unconditional forgiveness, but also to fully forgive himself for the poor choices he had made. Can you do that—completely accept God's forgiveness and forgive yourself? If you can, you're on your way to living a regret-free life.

One word of caution: When you go to God to express your sorrow over the things you've done, examine your heart first to be sure yours is a godly sorrow. What is it that you regret—getting caught or disappointing God? What are you truly experiencing—embarrassment in the presence of other people or repentance in the presence of God? Whenever you go to God hoping to experience forgiveness, you must go in total integrity, willing to expose your sinful heart to Him so He can replace it with a clean heart.

Do you still have regrets? The good news is that many decisions can be reversed; you can get off the wrong path that you've been taking through your decisions and start walking on the right path that God is wanting you to take. Have you made a decision that can't be reversed? There's good news in that situation as well. Though you'll have to live with the consequences, God can free you from living with regret if you'll only trust Him to lavish His wisdom and His joy on you.

Stop replaying the mental tapes of the mistakes you've made; all those instant replays will only make you miserable. Learn to live in the present as Paul did, by forgetting the past and pressing on to the future. When you let go of regret, you can face the coming years with excitement and expectancy for what God has in store for you.

I Will

Trust God to help me make decisions that I won't regret later.

    yes   *no*

Realize that the things I do today will play a part in shaping my life for years to come.

    yes   *no*

Face the future with excitement and expectancy.

    yes   *no*

Learn to live in the present.

    yes   *no*

Reverse a bad decision as soon as I realize I've made one.

    yes   *no*

Stop mentally replaying the mistakes I've made.

    yes   *no*

Things to Do

☐ Resolve to seek God's wisdom and the counsel of others for the life-changing decisions you'll face in the coming years.

☐ Read an account of Paul's life before and after his dramatic conversion to see how he was able to erase any regret for the sins of his past.

☐ Memorize Isaiah 43:18–19 or another verse on the next two pages. Better yet, memorize all of them!

☐ Make a poster for your bedroom that reads: "Will I regret this decision in the future?"

☐ Help a friend let go of the regret they're wallowing in.

Things to Remember

If we confess our sins, He is faithful and just to forgive us our sins and to cleanse us from all unrighteousness.

1 JOHN 1:9 NKJV

The weapons of our warfare are not carnal but mighty in God for pulling down strongholds, casting down arguments and every high thing that exalts itself against the knowledge of God, bringing every thought into captivity to the obedience of Christ.

2 CORINTHIANS 10:4–5 NKJV

Be renewed in the spirit of your mind.

—EPHESIANS 4:23 NKJV

How far has the LORD taken our sins from us? Farther than the distance from east to west.

PSALM 103:12 CEV

Do not remember the former things, nor consider the things of old. Behold, I will do a new thing, now it shall spring forth; shall you not know it? I will even make a road in the wilderness and rivers in the desert.

ISAIAH 43:18–19 NKJV

He has made everything beautiful in its time. Also He has put eternity in their hearts, except that no one can find out the work that God does from beginning to end.

ECCLESIASTES 3:11 NKJV

A voice from heaven said, "God will wipe away every tear from their eyes; there shall be no more death, nor sorrow, nor crying. There shall be no more pain, for the former things have passed away."

REVELATION 21:4 NKJV

Godly sorrow brings repentance that leads to salvation and leaves no regret, but worldly sorrow brings death.

2 CORINTHIANS 7:10 NIV

Repent therefore and be converted, that your sins may be blotted out, so that times of refreshing may come from the presence of the Lord.

ACTS 3:19 NKJV

Sing, O heavens! Be joyful, O earth! And break out in singing, O mountains! For the Lord has comforted His people, and will have mercy on His afflicted.

ISAIAH 49:13 NKJV

Go to the effort. Invest the time. Write the letter. Make the apology. Take the trip. Purchase the gift. Do it. The seized opportunity renders joy. The neglected brings regret.

—MAX LUCADO

Nobody who ever gave his best regretted it.

—GEORGE HALAS

Life Worth Living

A wise man will hear and increase learning, and a man of understanding will attain wise counsel

—Proverbs 1:5 NKJV

If you could ask God for anything in the world—anything at all—what would it be? A million dollars? A carefree existence? The love of your life? An ancient king once asked God for wisdom, and it seems he got more than his share—he became known as the wisest man in the world, and people came from all over the map just to listen to his wise sayings. King Solomon was certainly no mental midget even before he asked for wisdom—after all, he had the sense to ask for something that he would benefit from every day for the rest of his life. Fortunately, he wrote down much of what he received from God, and you now have access to it. Tucked in your Bible, just after the book of Psalms, is one of the greatest sources of wisdom you'll ever find—the book of Proverbs.

Before you begin reading, you might want to think a bit about just what wisdom is. The dictionary will tell you that wisdom is the "ability to discern inner qualities and relationships; insight; good sense; judgment." That's pretty good as far as it goes, but there's more to it than that — because the kind of wisdom you need to ask God for is heavenly wisdom, not worldly wisdom. Heavenly wisdom comes directly from the Father and produces righteousness and peace. Heavenly wisdom is pure and courteous, merciful, wholehearted, and sincere. It's straightforward and direct, and it accomplishes good things. Contrast all that with worldly wisdom, which gets filtered through the cultural standards of the day and produces evil and confusion. Worldly wisdom is just plain foolishness to God's way of thinking.

Now that you've got all that straight, it's time to get started in the book of Proverbs. Here's a taste of what you can expect to find as you work your way through the book: Insights that will enable you to discern between right and wrong. Warnings about the many pitfalls that await you on your journey through life. A strong dose of common sense for those who lack it. Guidelines for treating other people fairly. Strategies for dealing with the everyday problems of life. Principles to help you avoid making foolish decisions. Characteristics of a godly man and a godly woman. A greater measure of wisdom for those who are already wise. Practical advice for young people — just like you.

Like Solomon, though, you have to be smart enough to desire wisdom in order to make the most of your reading. Look at it this way. There are really only two ways to acquire wisdom — by making tons of foolish mistakes on your own through years of trial and error or by drawing on the wisdom of God and the people who have gone before you and learned their lessons well. Solomon fits into that second category, and you're fortunate to have his book to learn from. Couple your reading of Proverbs with prayer, and you've got a winning combination that will provide a significant boost to your spiritual growth.

Everything you do, every decision you make, every relationship you have, will be affected by your ability to apply wisdom to your experiences. When you have a deep understanding of why people behave the way they do—or of the underlying causes of certain problems, of the way seemingly isolated events can have an impact on each other, or of the consequences of specific actions—then you have acquired a level of understanding well beyond your years. Yours can be the voice of reason in an illogical situation. You can be the peacemaker whose understanding of both sides of an issue can lead to a satisfactory compromise. You can cut through the nonsense and get to the heart of a matter. Your wisdom will earn you respect and the right to be heard—despite your youth.

The book of James makes the promise that you can have exactly what Solomon acquired—heavenly wisdom, which is more precious than gold and silver—if only you will ask for it. Ask God for wisdom, and He will freely grant it to you. Ask God for wisdom in specific situations, and He will freely give you specific guidance. A gift of immeasurable value.

I Will

Trust God to help me acquire wisdom.   yes ____ no ____

Expect to grow spiritually as I draw on the
wisdom that comes from above.   yes ____ no ____

Search the scriptures for other insights into
wisdom.   yes ____ no ____

Draw on the wisdom of those who have gone
before me.   yes ____ no ____

Be open to new ways of looking at people,
events, and situations, based on my reading of
Proverbs.   yes ____ no ____

Things to Do

☐ Ask God for wisdom, just as Solomon did.

☐ Set up a system to remind yourself to read a chapter of Proverbs each
day, corresponding to the day of the month (that is, on the third day of
each month, read Proverbs 3 and so forth).

☐ Choose one current problem you have (such as anger or finances) and
find out what Proverbs has to say about it.

☐ Meditate on the scriptures and quotes on the following pages.

☐ In your own words, write out what you understand wisdom to be. Make
sure you have it clear in your mind.

Things to Remember

The fear of the LORD is the beginning of wisdom; a good understanding have all those who do His commandments. His praise endures forever.

PSALM 111:10 NKJV

Jesus said, "Settle it in your hearts not to meditate beforehand on what you will answer; for I will give you a mouth and wisdom which all your adversaries will not be able to contradict or resist."

LUKE 21:14–15 NKJV

His divine power has given to us all things that pertain to life and godliness, through the knowledge of Him who called us by glory and virtue.

—2 PETER 1:3 NKJV

The wisdom that comes from heaven is first of all.

JAMES 3:17 TLB

He who walks with wise men will be wise, but the companion of fools will be destroyed.

PROVERBS 13:20 NKJV

If any of you lacks wisdom, let him ask of God, who gives to all liberally and without reproach, and it will be given to him.

JAMES 1:5 NKJV

Let no one deceive himself. If anyone among you seems to be wise in this age, let him become a fool that he may become wise. For the wisdom of this world is foolishness with God. For it is written, "He catches the wise in their own craftiness."

1 CORINTHIANS 3:18–19 NKJV

The LORD gives wisdom; from His mouth come knowledge and understanding.

PROVERBS 2:6 NASB

How much better to get wisdom than gold! And to get understanding is to be chosen rather than silver.

PROVERBS 16:16 NKJV

Wisdom is the principal thing; therefore get wisdom. And in all your getting, get understanding.

PROVERBS 4:7 NKJV

Knowledge comes, but wisdom lingers.

—ALFRED, LORD TENNYSON

The wisdom of philosophy is completely revealed by God and given to philosophers; and it is he who illumines the souls of men in all wisdom.

—ROGER BACON

Wanting It All

Let us not become conceited, provoking one another,
envying one another.

—Galatians 5:26 NKJV

Your buddy Dave got the most incredible cherry-red
sports car over summer vacation, and you could hardly
stand to be around him whenever he started talking about
it. But that was nothing compared to the way you felt
when Nick—the guy who stole your girlfriend last year—
drove up in a brand-new four-wheel drive. Him, you
wanted to clobber. You secretly hoped his Jeep would be
repossessed and they'd reopen debtor's prison just for his
sorry self.

So what's the verdict here on your bad-attitude
charges? Guilty of one count of jealousy, in the matter of
your buddy Dave. Guilty of one count of jealousy and one
count of envy, in the matter of your sorry enemy Nick. In
both matters laid out before the godly court, you wanted
something you couldn't have, something that belonged to
someone else. That's jealousy. Think of it as a
misdemeanor, something of a lesser charge. But in the

matter of Nick, you also wanted to do him bodily harm and deprive him of his wheels, all four of them. This is a more serious charge, closely akin to a felony.

Now that you're a spiritually convicted felon, what will you do about it? Plead before the court for mercy, of course. And God will forgive you and extend His mercy to you. But it's your responsibility to deal with the root problem: wanting it all. Not only the sports car and the four-wheel drive but also the pain and suffering of a guy named Nick. Give it up. You'll never have it all. You'll never even have most of it all. So plead with the court for one more favor, the gift of contentment. That's another gift that God will gladly give you; be prepared to accept it.

The irony here is that in one sense, you already have it all—everything you need in life, in the person of Jesus Christ. So maybe you can't use Him to impress your friends as you drive around town. But His light shining through your life will draw the right kind of onlookers, those whose hearts are aching for the kind of love He offers.

Jealousy and envy threaten to destroy your relationships, rob you of peace and joy, and keep your focus glued to material things. Godly contentment takes your eyes off of things and returns your focus where it belongs: on God and the people around you who need to see the light of Christ in your satisfied life.

I Will

Keep my focus on God and those who need to see
His love through me.

yes _no_

Allow others to see the light of Christ in me by
giving up my jealous and envious feelings.

yes _no_

Understand that I have everything I need in the
person of Jesus Christ.

yes _no_

Expect God to show me how to be content with
what I have.

yes _no_

Begin to repair the relationships I've damaged by
my bad attitudes.

yes _no_

Things to Do

☐ Confess your feelings of jealousy and envy to God.

☐ Read the story of Joseph and his brothers in Genesis 37 for an eye-
opening account of the kind of behavior that jealousy and envy can
lead to.

☐ Think of a recent incident that stirred up jealous feelings within you.
Decide how you could have handled the situation in a more mature way.

☐ Memorize Hebrews 13:5.

☐ There's a positive side to jealousy. Read about it in 2 Corinthians 11:2–3.

Things to Remember

Let your conduct be without covetousness; be content with such things as you have. For He Himself has said, "I will never leave you nor forsake you."

HEBREWS 13:5 NKJV

Love suffers long and is kind; love does not envy; love does not parade itself, is not puffed up.

1 CORINTHIANS 13:4 NKJV

The effects of the corrupt nature are obvious: illicit sex, perversion, promiscuity, idolatry, drug use, hatred, rivalry, jealousy, angry outbursts, selfish ambition, conflict, factions, envy, drunkenness, wild partying, and similar things. I've told you in the past and I'm telling you again that people who do these kinds of things will not inherit the kingdom of God.

GALATIANS 5:19–21 GOD'S WORD

You are still carnal. For where there are envy, strife, and divisions among you, are you not carnal and behaving like mere men?

1 CORINTHIANS 3:3 NKJV

Envy takes the joy, happiness, and contentment out of living.

BILLY GRAHAM

They that envy others are their inferiors.

AUTHOR UNKNOWN

Danger Zone

We do not have a High Priest who cannot sympathize with our weaknesses, but was in all points tempted as we are, yet without sin. Let us therefore come boldly to the throne of grace, that we may obtain mercy and find grace to help in time of need.

—*Hebrews 4:15–16 NKJV*

Ah, what a great morning! You wake up in time to get dressed, eat a really good breakfast, and even spend a few minutes in prayer and Bible reading. You grab your schoolbooks and head for the front door. You turn the knob, the door opens, and you step outside. But watch out! You've just entered the Danger Zone.

Day in and day out, you're surrounded by temptation, even if the inside of your house has been swept clean of every influence that could tempt you to sin. Once you step outside, it's as if you're in the middle of the North Atlantic, with icy mountains of temptation scattered across the horizon. In the course of a single day, you'll have more opportunities to lie, cheat, and steal than you ever thought possible. And that's just the tip of the iceberg. The pile of hidden temptations is big enough to sink the *Titanic*.

Fortunately, you're stronger than the *Titanic* if you remember to give your day, with all its temptations, to God when you pray each morning. And if you've been faithful to stay in close contact with the Father all throughout the day, then you have such a sensitive radar system that you can spot the iceberg of sin looming in your path in plenty of time to change your course. You also have the wisdom to know that the icebergs will always be out there, and an immediate course correction is the only way to avoid them.

Maybe you're not such a great navigator yet. All this is so new to you. How on earth—or on sea—can you handle the myriad temptations in your way? You learn from the Master, the one who stood on a mountaintop and stared temptation down. With each temptation that Satan offered Him, Jesus struck a devastating blow, quoting from the Word of God. "It is written," He said, reciting a definitive verse from the scriptures. Satan could not withstand the truth. He left Jesus alone and took his bag of sinful temptations with him.

Temptation is unavoidable. The way you handle temptation is what will make the difference in your spiritual track record. With some really fast running shoes and an arsenal of memorized scripture, you can flee temptation and wage a verbal counterattack at the same time. With each victory you'll build up your resistance to temptation and no longer fear the moment you have to step out into the Danger Zone.

I Will

Remember to give my day to God each morning. _____ yes _____ no

Place a high priority on memorizing scripture so I'll
be prepared for Satan's attacks. _____ yes _____ no

Flee temptation as soon as I recognize it. _____ yes _____ no

Realize that I cannot avoid temptation, but I can
avoid giving in to it. _____ yes _____ no

Trust God to make me sensitive to the first signs of
temptation. _____ yes _____ no

Learn how to resist Satan by following Jesus'
example. _____ yes _____ no

Things to Do

☐ Read the account of Jesus' temptation by Satan in Matthew 4.

☐ Identify the greatest temptations in your life right now. Eliminate
anything that feeds that temptation (certain videos, for instance).

☐ Memorize 1 Corinthians 10:13. It's a great verse to remember when you're
tempted. (Remember to look for the way of escape!)

☐ Post a reminder—someplace where you're sure to see it each morning—
to ask God to help you resist temptation.

☐ Recall the last time you gave in to temptation. See if you can now
identify the "way of escape" God had provided for you.

Things to Remember

Jesus said, "Watch and pray, lest you enter into temptation. The spirit indeed is willing, but the flesh is weak."

MARK 14:38 NKJV

Ponder the path of your feet, and let all your ways be established. Do not turn to the right or the left; remove your foot from evil.

PROVERBS 4:26–27 NKJV

How can a young man cleanse his way? By taking heed according to Your word.

PSALM 119:9 NKJV

No testing has overtaken you that is not common to everyone. God is faithful, and he will not let you be tested beyond your strength, but with the testing he will also provide the way out so that you may be able to endure it.

1 CORINTHIANS 10:13 NRSV

Humble yourselves before God. Resist the Devil, and he will flee from you.

JAMES 4:7 NLT

· ·

Most people who fly from temptation usually leave a forwarding address.

AUTHOR UNKNOWN

Temptation is the fire that brings up the scum of the heart.

THOMAS BOSTON

Moving Mountains

Jesus said, "I say to you, if you have faith as a mustard seed, you will say to this mountain, 'Move from here to there,' and it will move; and nothing will be impossible for you."

—Matthew 17:20 NKJV

Maybe you've heard the tale about the ancient king who placed a boulder in the middle of a road. Everyone took the long way around it, all the while complaining about the king's failure to maintain the highways, until a lowly peasant came along and pushed the boulder out of the way. Where the boulder had been he found a purse filled with gold coins, a gift from the king intended for the person who removed the boulder. The moral of the story? Every obstacle offers the possibility of improving your lot in life.

What about you? Are you like the complainers who take the long way around an obstacle? Or are you like the one person who removed the obstacle and found a better life in its place? Maybe you don't think you have the strength to move the boulders that are blocking your path right now, but you know the One who does. And He once said that if you have even the tiniest measure of faith, you can move mountains. A boulder is nothing to Him!

Genuine faith in God is an overcoming faith. It's a faith that does not make a U-turn when it faces a boulder in the road, nor does it take the long way around. It's a faith that knows how to cut to the chase, because faith in God is an active faith that gets things done. It's the kind of faith that enables an elderly woman to bear a child, breaks down prison doors so the captives can go free, and renders the bite of a venomous snake completely harmless—just three of the many accounts of overcoming faith found in the Bible.

No matter what is standing in your way right now, God is big enough to remove it. And He'll do it, if the way you're traveling is the course He has set you on. If the boulder between you and college is tuition, trust Him to provide the funds at just the right time. Maybe the biggest obstacle in your life is failure to communicate with your parents. Trust God; He invented communication. Can't find a job? God loves work! Trust Him to lead you to the right job.

Are you getting the picture? The way to overcome obstacles is by activating your faith in God. Take whatever measure of faith you have right now and trust God to move the boulder in your life. In its place, you just may find a life-changing treasure.

I Will

Trust God to remove the obstacles in my life.   yes   no

Focus on God, not on the obstacles.   yes   no

Learn to see obstacles as opportunities.   yes   no

Make sure I'm on the right path when I call on
God to move the boulder in my way.   yes   no

Realize that even the smallest amount of faith can
accomplish great results.   yes   no

Be thankful for the opportunities I have to activate
my faith.   yes   no

Things to Do

☐ Read the accounts of overcoming faith mentioned in Genesis 21, Acts 16, and Acts 28.

☐ Identify the biggest obstacle in your life right now. Give it to God and imagine Him rolling it out of your path.

☐ Memorize Matthew 17:20.

☐ Meditate on what it means to activate your faith.

☐ Thank God for giving you the kind of faith that can move mountains.

☐ Write an account of all the obstacles God has removed from your life so far.

Things to Remember

Whatever is born of God overcomes the world. And this is the victory that has overcome the world—our faith.

1 JOHN 5:4 NKJV

Even the youths shall faint and be weary, and the young men shall utterly fall, but those who wait on the LORD shall renew their strength; they shall mount up with wings like eagles, they shall run and not be weary, they shall walk and not faint.

ISAIAH 40:30–31 NKJV

It has become evident to the whole palace guard, and to all the rest, that my chains are in Christ; and most of the brethren in the Lord, having become confident by my chains, are much more bold to speak the word without fear.

PHILIPPIANS 1:13–14 NKJV

In all these things we overwhelmingly conquer through Him who loved us.

ROMANS 8:37 NASB

He did not say, "You shall not be tempted; you shall not be travailed; you shall not be afflicted." But he said, "You shall not be overcome."

SAINT JULIAN OF NORWICH

The Promised Land always lies on the other side of a wilderness.

HAVELOCK ELLIS

CHEERFULNESS

Can't Hurt

All the days of the afflicted are evil, but he who is of a merry heart has a continual feast.

—*Proverbs 15:15* NKJV

Here's a good one for you: Go through whatever teen or young adult magazines you have lying around the house and try to find an advertisement featuring a cheerful model. Warning: This may take some time. In fact, this may be Mission Impossible. For whatever reason, adopting a defiant, pouty, or just plain miserable attitude has become chic. The worst offenders are rock bands, including some Christian groups. Check out the CD covers—does anyone appear to be even slightly happy, let alone joyful? What's baffling is that when you see these same performers in concert or on a talk show, they're clearly enjoying themselves.

Now that you know that their trendy attitude is all a put-on, you can breathe a sigh of relief and stop trying to conform to the false image they've been conveying. Constantly wearing an expression of gloom and doom can eventually deceive you into believing that your life really is gloomy and doomed. So ditch the pouty persona and start telling yourself the truth, that it's OK to be cheerful. Look at it this way: It can't hurt. And you have an awful lot to be cheerful about.

One surefire way to transform your countenance into a cheerful one is to start singing praises to God. Go ahead—you can do it! If you've never sung praises to God on your own before, it might feel awkward at first. But once you've done it for a while, you'll become so comfortable with it that you'll be hearing praise songs in your head while you're at school or playing basketball or flipping burgers. And you know what? The joy that's in your spirit will show on your face.

Wouldn't you like to be known as a person who can light up a room just by entering it? That sounds so enchanting; it's the type of compliment that you believe should be reserved for the likes of Julia Roberts. Your smile may not be as big as hers, but it can still light up a room. And it can create a healthy buzz about you: What's her secret? they'll start asking, or How can he be so pleasant all the time? You know the answer. What better way to tell others about Jesus?

Your face reflects the condition of your heart. If your heart isn't joyful, there's a problem in your relationship with God. Ask Him how to fix it—and be prepared to do a whole lot of smiling when the repair work is over.

I Will

Remind myself that my cheerfulness is a positive
witness for Christ.

      yes   no

Be more cheerful in my attitude and my
appearance.

      yes   no

Ignore the chic trend to appear defiant.

      yes   no

Realize that the expression on my face reflects
the condition of my heart.

      yes   no

Cultivate a joyful heart.

      yes   no

Things to Do

☐ Smile. Right now. For no reason at all.

☐ Ask God to help you be more cheerful.

☐ Make a list of the praise songs you know. Keep the list in your Bible so
you'll never be at a loss for a song to sing.

☐ Write a letter to a Christian band asking why their CD covers don't
reflect the joy of knowing Jesus. Send the letter. Rejoice if you get a
response!

☐ Memorize Proverbs 15:15. After all, who doesn't like food?

☐ For the next three days, be cheerful whenever you're around your
parents.

Things to Remember

Praise the LORD! Praise the LORD, O my soul! While I live I will praise the LORD; I will sing praises to my God while I have my being.

PSALM 146:1–2 NKJV

Anyone who is having troubles should pray. Anyone who is happy should sing praises.

JAMES 5:13 NCV

When you eat the labor of your hands, you shall be happy, and it shall be well with you.

PSALM 128:2 NKJV

Every man according as he purposeth in his heart, so let him give; not grudgingly, or of necessity: for God loveth a cheerful giver.

2 CORINTHIANS 9:7 KJV

Praise the LORD! Praise, O servants of the LORD, praise the name of the LORD! Blessed be the name of the LORD from this time forth and forevermore! From the rising of the sun to its going down the LORD's name is to be praised.

PSALM 113:1–3 NKJV

· ·

Health and cheerfulness mutually beget each other.

JOSEPH ADDISON

Hope is the power of being cheerful in circumstances we know to be desperate.

G. K. CHESTERTON

Go Figure

My God shall supply all your need according to His riches in glory by Christ Jesus.

—*Philippians 4:19* NKJV

It's tough being a teenager and listening to adults talk about how money can't buy happiness and how you need to be frugal and how you shouldn't strive to be wealthy. After all, you've never even had any real money, just pocket change at best.

They don't lay off because they know that they'd be doing you a disservice. Most adults know that if you learn to handle money when you're young, you have a greater shot at handling it well for the rest of your life. That's what you want, isn't it? The things they're advising you to do now will pay off in the future. You've probably heard it all: Tithe religiously. Give freely. Spend cautiously. Save abundantly. Invest carefully. Budget regularly. It's all good advice. But these are just starting points.

What you need to do is develop a healthy attitude toward money. Money can be your servant or your master, and you get to choose which one it will be. Let's say you make the right choice and decree that money will be your servant from now on. Now you're on a roll. Your servant is there to meet your needs and to help finance God's work. Your servant enables you to live a life of contentment and joy and never threatens to usurp God's place in your life.

If you allow money to become the master of your life, watch out! You'll never have enough. You'll waste your life worrying about how much you have and how much you want to have and how to keep it secure. Since you can't serve two masters, there goes your opportunity to serve God. You'll end up buying things, things, and more things to try to restore the joy you once knew in the presence of God. All that stuff will rob you of time and energy, as you dust it, clean it, maintain it, repair it, store it, display it, and move it from house to house for the rest of your life. Pretty depressing prospects for the future, wouldn't you say?

You can handle your money wisely and still have fun with it, as long as you keep it in its position of servitude. Let your money work for you and for God. Be a good steward of your finances today—even if your assets total only $3.52, safely tucked away in a piggy bank.

I Will

Place a high priority on God's work when it comes
to spending my money.   yes ___   no ___

Avoid financial disaster by drawing on God's
wisdom and the advice of others.   yes ___   no ___

Allow God to have control over my finances.   yes ___   no ___

Make money my servant and not my master.   yes ___   no ___

Develop a healthy attitude toward money.   yes ___   no ___

Find contentment in life, not in things.   yes ___   no ___

Things to Do

☐ Officially make God the master of your finances. Ask Him to give you
wisdom for the financial decisions you have to make.

☐ Look up the word stewardship using an online study Bible and read the
corresponding verses.

☐ Keep a log of how much money you spend in a week. Don't forget all
those coins you feed to vending machines.

☐ The following week, try to break your record by spending less.

☐ Count up all the money you have right now. Tithe on it, even if your
tithe only amounts to 35 cents from that piggy bank of yours.

Things to Remember

God is the one who gives seed to the farmer and then bread to eat. In the same way, he will give you many opportunities to do good, and he will produce a great harvest of generosity in you. Yes, you will be enriched so that you can give even more generously. And when we take your gifts to those who need them, they will break out in thanksgiving to God.

2 CORINTHIANS 9:10–11 NLT

A good man leaves an inheritance to his children's children, but the wealth of the sinner is stored up for the righteous.

PROVERBS 13:22 NKJV

In the Parable of the Talents, Jesus said, "Well done, good and faithful servant; you have been faithful over a few things, I will make you ruler over many things. Enter into the joy of your lord."

MATTHEW 25:23 NKJV

The love of money is at the root of all kinds of evil. And some people, craving money, have wandered from the faith and pierced themselves with many sorrows.

1 TIMOTHY 6:10 NLT

When I have any money I get rid of it as quickly as possible, lest it find a way into my heart.

JOHN WESLEY

Money spent on myself may be a millstone about my neck; money spent on others may give me wings like the angels.

ROSWELL DWIGHT HITCHCOCK

Wild Blue Yonder

God has not given us a spirit of fear, but of power and of love and of a sound mind.

—2 Timothy 1:7 NKJV

There you are, sitting in your guidance counselor's office for the umpteenth time, listening to her talk about how you're college material and you have all this potential and what a waste it would be if you didn't at least give it a try. *I don't know*, you're thinking. *Maybe she's right. But I just don't think I could cut it at college. I'm not sure I have what it takes.* Time will tell whether you have what it takes, but right now it's pretty obvious what you don't have: a healthy measure of self-confidence.

There's no valid reason for a Christian to lack confidence. Sure, you shouldn't walk around acting as if you can conquer the world and crush everybody in it, but neither should you doubt your own abilities. You're not only a precious human being made in the image of God, you're also a spiritually regenerated person, which simply means you've been born again into the family of God. You really can do all things through Christ who strengthens you.

Just watch out when people try to convince you that you can be anything you want to be. That's, well, a lie. It simply is not true. Believing in yourself doesn't mean that you can be a world-famous doctor if you can't stand the sight of blood, or a top-notch lawyer if you hate to argue in defense of an issue. You'll only experience frustration if you believe in yourself without believing in the One who created you and following the path He has chosen for you. He knows you better than you know yourself, and He will lead you to become the person He knows you can be.

If you're having problems with self-confidence, you probably need to hand over your self-esteem to God. He's the expert at those kinds of repairs, and He'll have you believing in yourself in no time. He wants your self-esteem to be healthy, because He knows you'll never meet your spiritual potential until it is.

From now on, listen to what God has to say about you. He thinks you're pretty terrific, and He knows you can do all kinds of things that you can't even imagine doing at the moment. Let Him build your confidence and just see what happens then. But brace yourself: Not even the sky is the limit where He's concerned!

I Will

Allow God to restore my self-confidence.   yes ___ no ___

Believe that I can do all things through Christ.   yes ___ no ___

Pay close attention to God's opinion of me.   yes ___ no ___

Get rid of anything that hinders my spiritual
growth.   yes ___ no ___

Understand that healthy confidence is not the
same as unhealthy conceit.   yes ___ no ___

Expect God to enable me to do things I can't even
imagine.   yes ___ no ___

Things to Do

☐ Make a list of all the things you could do if you really believed
Philippians 4:13.

☐ Hand your self-esteem over to God to make whatever repairs are
necessary.

☐ Ask God to forgive you for doubting the abilities He gave you.

☐ Look in a mirror and say, "God thinks I'm terrific!" Then say it again.

☐ Try doing something new—something you used to tell yourself
that you couldn't possibly do.

☐ Read Psalm 139.

Things to Remember

Ananias told Saul, "The God of our fathers has chosen you that you should know His will, and see the Just One, and hear the voice of His mouth."

ACTS 22:14 NKJV

As many as are led by the Spirit of God, these are sons of God.

ROMANS 8:14 NKJV

Little children, you are from God, and have conquered them; for the one who is in you is greater than the one who is in the world.

1 JOHN 4:4 NRSV

I can do all things through Christ who strengthens me.

PHILIPPIANS 4:13 NKJV

Paul wrote: I bow my knees to the Father of our Lord Jesus Christ… that He would grant you, according to the riches of His glory, to be strengthened with might through His Spirit in the inner man.

EPHESIANS 3:14 NKJV

• •

We have to take ourselves, good and bad alike, on trust before we can do anything.

MARTIN ISRAEL

A humble knowledge of yourself is a surer way to God than an extensive search after learning.

THOMAS À KEMPIS

Making a Comeback

Beloved, do not avenge yourselves, but rather give place to wrath; for it is written, "Vengeance is Mine, I will repay," says the Lord.

—*Romans 12:19 NKJV*

Dave overhears you telling Paul that you've finally worked up the nerve to ask Holly to the prom, and the next thing you know, he goes and asks her first. You can't believe it! Dave, of all people! Well, he's just landed a secure spot on your ex-friend list.

But that's not quite enough; you really want to make him pay for this. You feel like a boxer who's ready to make his comeback after a humiliating defeat. You want your opponent to suffer big-time. Your mind races with devious schemes for getting back at him. Most involve bodily harm—the kind that would keep him out of the way until after prom night. You want revenge, and plenty of it.

The urge to exact revenge is perfectly normal; giving in to that urge is perfectly awful. Whatever satisfaction you may get from it will be so short-lived that you'll wonder why you thought it was such a good idea in the first place. And then you'll begin to feel perfectly miserable.

Instead of exacting revenge, try doing good by offering forgiveness. Until you forgive an offender, your hardened heart—the Bible calls this a "stony" heart—fills up with anger and bitterness—not just toward the offender, but also toward others and even yourself. *Why did I have to go open my big mouth with Dave standing right behind me? Why didn't I ask Holly sooner?* you wonder, beating yourself up by second-guessing. Does this sound like a fun way to live?

Forgiveness heals. When you forgive others, the open wounds they inflict on you begin to close up—and the bruises you give yourself begin to fade. Eventually, the sore spots disappear altogether. And God will make good on His promise to replace your hard and stony heart with a softened heart that beats with new life.

By the way, if you're tempted to suddenly get biblical and start quoting the "eye for an eye" verse from Exodus 21, you might want to know that God intended that to be a standard for the court system, not an excuse for personal retribution. God came right out and laid it on the line: "Vengeance is Mine"—not yours. You want to see vengeance? Nobody can do vengeance like God can. Keep your mitts off the situation, forgive the offender, and let God handle it. He'll do a much better job, and you won't end up feeling perfectly miserable.

I Will

Trust God to handle offenses on my behalf.

_____ yes _____ no

Put the healing power of forgiveness to the test whenever I'm offended.

_____ yes _____ no

Allow God to soften my hard heart.

_____ yes _____ no

Recognize the desire for revenge and squelch it immediately.

_____ yes _____ no

Remember that only God has the authority to seek vengeance.

_____ yes _____ no

Learn to forgive those who hurt me instead of to want revenge.

_____ yes _____ no

Things to Do

☐ Give your heart of stone to God so He can soften it.

☐ Read Matthew 5:39–45 to see what the Lord expects you to do to avoid exacting revenge.

☐ Read several biblical accounts of revenge that backfired, such as 2 Samuel 3:22–39; 1 Kings 22:24–38; the story of Haman throughout the book of Esther; Ezekiel 25.

☐ There's a saying that suggests you dig two graves before setting out on a journey of revenge. In your journal, write about how this warning can apply to your life.

☐ Memorize Matthew 5:44.

Things to Remember

Jesus said, "I say to you, love your enemies, bless those who curse you, do good to those who hate you, and pray for those who spitefully use you and persecute you."

MATTHEW 5:44 NKJV

The LORD said, "I will give you a new heart and put a new spirit within you; I will take the heart of stone out of your flesh and give you a heart of flesh."

EZEKIEL 36:26 NKJV

Do not say, "I will recompense evil;" wait for the LORD, and He will save you.

PROVERBS 20:22 NKJV

Jesus said, "Will not God bring about justice for his chosen ones, who cry out to him day and night? Will he keep putting them off? I tell you, he will see that they get justice, and quickly. However, when the Son of Man comes, will he find faith on the earth?"

LUKE 18:7–8 NIV

See that no one renders evil for evil to anyone, but always pursue what is good both for yourselves and for all.

1 THESSALONIANS 5:15 NKJV

· ·

There is no revenge so complete as forgiveness.

JOSH BILLINGS

Never does the human soul appear so strong and noble as when it forgoes revenge and dares to forgive an injury.

EDWIN HUBBEL CHAPIN

Taking the Heat

*You are inexcusable, O man, whoever you are who judge,
for in whatever you judge another you condemn yourself;
for you who judge practice the same things.*

—Romans 2:1 NKJV

Imagine yourself standing at the pearly gates, trying
to explain why you should be allowed to enter. Of course,
in this scenario, you'd look old, since you have no
intention of reaching those gates until you're 85 at the
youngest. As you stand there, you're confronted with a
few minor details, like the fact that you never gave
yourself wholeheartedly to God and never really repented
of your sins and trusted Jesus.

Your side of the conversation goes something like this:
"Well, I really didn't hear about Jesus until I was in high
school, where everybody thought the Christian kids were
dorky, and then, what with college and getting married
and having kids and starting a business and all that—well,
you know how it is. I mean, I went to church pretty often
and there were times when I wanted to respond to the
gospel, but everyone was looking and, well, you've got to

take into account all the money I gave to charity, right? Look, I've been busy. I wanted to clean my act up first. If You hadn't made life so complicated, I would have had more time for You..." Now you've done it! You ran out of excuses, so you started blaming God for the very life He gave you—the one you should have given back to Him all along.

Not a pretty picture, is it? If you could ask God how many excuses He's heard over the millennia, He'd quote a number so high that your eyes would glaze over as your brain tried in vain to process it. And if you asked what some of those excuses were, you'd no doubt hear some doozies, like the old "the dog ate my Bible" kind of thing. You can be sure that God has heard it all, and it's unlikely that you'll come up with that one excuse that will be so dazzling that He won't notice as you surreptitiously slip through the gates.

Better to get your act together here and now. So what if the kids think Christians are dorky? You can be the one to prove them wrong! So what if everyone's looking when you feel prompted to respond to the gospel? That just makes for a bigger celebration! And excuses about the lack of time and the complexities of life? People have been using those excuses since the dawn of history and the invention of the wheel.

OK, so now you know what you have to do just in case you're not really sure about your eternal destination: You have to get sure! But even if you've settled the question about where you will spend eternity, you still need to be on guard against excuses. Moses gave so many excuses for his unwillingness to serve as God's spokesman that he really ticked God off. (You don't want to do that!) Then some of the early Christians came along and used Paul's teachings about grace and freedom as an excuse to continue in their lives of sin. "May it never be!" Paul said to them—and he says it to you as well.

May it never be that you would put off dedicating your life to Christ so you could have a little worldly fun while you're young. May it never be that you would grieve the heart of God by twisting His kind offer of grace and mercy into a self-serving excuse to gratify your desires. May it never be that you would reach an advanced age and realize that your life has been one long excuse for not serving the Father.

Once you've got that sorted out, you need to be on guard against all those times you start to make excuses for your behavior and actions in the here and now—at home, at school, at church, at your job, in any and all of your relationships. You probably won't get away with it anyway, since people can usually smell a rotten excuse a mile away.

Deep down, you know when you're about to utter some lame excuse when you find yourself in vat of hot water. Tell the truth, dry yourself off, and get back on track with God. Your garment of grace will never feel better.

I Will

Never use God's gift of grace as an excuse to
continue in sin. _yes_ _no_

Settle any spiritual issues in my life immediately. _yes_ _no_

Cherish my freedom in Christ by not abusing it. _yes_ _no_

Expect God's Spirit to alert me when I'm about to
make an excuse. _yes_ _no_

Learn to recognize those situations in which I most
often tend to make excuses. _yes_ _no_

Realize that I can't clean up my act without God's
help. _yes_ _no_

Things to Do

☐ Ask God to forgive you for the times you've used excuses to avoid
spending time with Him.

☐ Think about the last time you failed to do something you know you
should have done. Write down the excuses you gave—and then write
down the truth.

☐ Read Exodus 3:12—4:17 to see how God dealt with Moses' excuses and
lack of faith.

☐ Memorize Romans 1:20.

☐ Ask your parents to forgive you for a recent situation in which you
made an excuse for your behavior.

Things to Remember

Since the creation of the world His invisible attributes are clearly seen, being understood by the things that are made, even His eternal power and Godhead, so that they are without excuse.

ROMANS 1:20 NKJV

When they saw the boldness of Peter and John, and perceived that they were uneducated and untrained men, they marveled. And they realized that they had been with Jesus.

ACTS 4:13 NKJV

Jesus said, "If I had not come and spoken to them, they would have no sin, but now they have no excuse for their sin."

—JOHN 15:22 NKJV

What then shall we say to these things? If God is for us, who can be against us?

ROMANS 8:31 NKJV

My speech and my preaching were not with persuasive words of human wisdom, but in demonstration of the Spirit and of power, that your faith should not be in the wisdom of men but in the power of God.

1 CORINTHIANS 2:4–5 NKJV

The LORD said to him, "Who has made man's mouth? Or who makes the mute, the deaf, the seeing, or the blind? Have not I, the Lord? Now therefore, go, and I will be with your mouth and teach you what you shall say."

EXODUS 4:11–12 NKJV

In the Parable of the Dinner, Jesus said, "They all alike began to make excuses. The first one said to him, 'I have bought a piece of land and I need to go out and look at it; please consider me excused.' Another one said, 'I have bought five yoke of oxen, and I am going to try them out; please consider me excused.' Another one said, 'I have married a wife, and for that reason I cannot come.'"

LUKE 14:18–20 NASB

What shall we say then? Shall we continue in sin that grace may abound? Certainly not! How shall we who died to sin live any longer in it?

ROMANS 6:1–2 NKJV

You have been given freedom: not freedom to do wrong, but freedom to love and serve each other.

GALATIANS 5:13 TLB

Each of us must give an account to God for what we do.

ROMANS 14:12 CEV

Don't make excuses, make good.

—AUTHOR UNKNOWN

Ninety-nine percent of the failures come from people who have the habit of making excuses.

—GEORGE WASHINGTON CARVER

Strong Shoulders

Bear one another's burdens, and so fulfill the law of Christ.
—Galatians 6:2 NKJV

"It's not my problem!" How many times have you heard someone say that? How many times have you said that? Probably more times than you can count. It's true that you shouldn't make everyone else's problem your own; no one can carry the weight of their world on their shoulders. But you also shouldn't walk away from someone whose burden is much too heavy for one person to bear.

Whose burdens are too heavy to carry alone? The guy at school whose older brother is off fighting terrorism in some remote spot on the globe. The girl whose parents can't talk to each other without yelling. The kid in geometry class who never gets anything right. The friend whose fumble in the last quarter of the game lost the state championship. The family at church that just discovered that the mother has breast cancer. Different burdens, different degrees of seriousness. But in each case, there's a person who is weighed down by the crushing burden and who needs someone to help carry the load.

How can you help? Not by offering empty encouragement ("Just cheer up!") or false promises ("Your brother is going to be just fine!"). You can help by being there, ready and willing to chuck your plans for the afternoon if he or she needs someone to talk to—or to be with. Pray for that person and offer a shoulder to cry on.

Doesn't sound like much, does it? Maybe you've done all that for someone, and you didn't feel you had done enough. That's a fairly good indication that you were doing just what God wanted you to do. God has this amazing ability to take what you see as your puny efforts and transform them into a powerful action for good in another person's life. What's even more amazing, when you lighten another's load, you don't feel any of the weight that's been transferred to your shoulders; in fact, you'll probably feel lighter than ever.

By now, you've probably noticed more than a few paradoxes in the kingdom of God: To have, give; to become great, serve; to overcome revenge, forgive. This is simply another kingdom paradox: To lighten your load, lighten the load of another person. It may not be your problem, but you may be carrying a fair portion of the solution right on your own shoulders.

I Will

Ask God for wisdom to know which burdens are not
mine to carry.

yes _____ no _____

Realize that I can't take on the world's problems, but
I can help the people around me.

yes _____ no _____

Believe that God can do something powerful with my
puny efforts.

yes _____ no _____

Offer my shoulder for a friend to cry on.

yes _____ no _____

Expect my load to lighten as I help carry
someone else's.

yes _____ no _____

Be available when a friend needs someone to talk to.

yes _____ no _____

Things to Do

☐ Ask God to show you who in your life right now needs a friend the
most.

☐ Lighten a friend's load by offering to pray with him about a struggle
he's having.

☐ Thank God for enabling you to share in the concerns of another.

☐ All parents carry a heavy load. Figure out at least one thing you can do
to help your parents—and then do it.

☐ Memorize 1 John 3:16.

Things to Remember

We know love, because He laid down His life for us. And we also ought to lay down our lives for the brethren.

1 JOHN 3:16 NKJV

Two are better than one.... If they fall, one will lift up his companion. But woe to him who is alone when he falls, for he has no one to help him up.

ECCLESIASTES 4:9–10 NKJV

Jesus said, "Greater love has no one than this, than to lay down one's life for his friends."

JOHN 15:13 NKJV

Give your burdens to the LORD, he will take care of you. He will not permit the godly to slip and fall.

PSALM 55:22 NLT

Let [God] have all your worries and cares, for he is always thinking about you and watching everything that concerns you.

1 PETER 5:7 TLB

Though one may be overpowered by another, two can withstand him. And a threefold cord is not quickly broken.

ECCLESIASTES 4:12 NKJV

● ●

God gave burdens, also shoulders.

YIDDISH PROVERB

No one is useless in this world who lightens the burdens of another.

CHARLES DICKENS

Don't Sweat It

David said to the Philistine, "All this assembly shall know that the Lord does not save with sword and spear; for the battle is the Lord's, and He will give you into our hands."
—1 Samuel 17:47 NKJV

You've worked hard and trained like a maniac for months. No one has practiced shooting hoops more than you have—even the guys in the neighborhood say you're good at it, and they never say that about a girl! There's one spot left open on the girls' varsity basketball team, and you've claimed that spot for yourself, even if you're only a sophomore.

But when that final roster is announced, you're stunned—you didn't make it! Some junior got the last open slot on the team, and you know why. She just happens to be the daughter of a school board member. Favoritism, that's all it is! Just wait till you get home and tell your parents! That school is in for one big messy fight. Your parents will see to it that you get on the team.

Back away from the edge. Calm down. Take a deep breath and ask yourself a couple of questions: *Is this really worth fighting for? Will this matter five years from now? Do I want to play basketball—which I can do on the JV team—or do I want to look good by being the only sophomore on the varsity team?* If you choose to go ahead with this fight, you're in for a prolonged struggle that will accomplish little besides spreading bad feelings all around. As they say, no good can come from this.

With maturity and wisdom comes the ability to decide what is worth fighting for and what isn't. Some battles are obvious: Anything of eternal value is worth fighting to the death for; a no-brainer is a battle that isn't even worth taking time to think about. But then there are all those battles in between—struggles for personal rights or for important principles like fairness and justice. That's when you have to ask yourself the kinds of questions mentioned above.

So when is a battle worth it? There will be times when only you, with God's guidance, can decide that. If it is worth it, then you need to give it all you've got, to the point where you're willing to suffer whatever consequences result from your efforts—including going to jail or being injured or losing your job. If it's not worth it, don't sweat it. There's no point in wasting your time, energy, and witness for Christ on a struggle over trivial matters. Leave the battle to God and move on with your life.

I Will

Trust God to help me determine what is worth
fighting for and what isn't.

yes   *no*

Be willing to walk away from a pointless fight,
even when it hurts to do so.

yes   *no*

Have the courage to fight it out when eternal
consequences are at stake.

yes   *no*

Keep a cool head no matter what kind of battle
I'm engaged in.

yes   *no*

Have a mature attitude toward the battles I face.

yes   *no*

Strive to be known as a peacemaker.

yes   *no*

Things to Do

☐ Ask God to reveal to you any areas in your life in which you tend to
make a big deal over trivial issues.

☐ Memorize Romans 12:17–18.

☐ Copy Norman Vincent Peale's quotation at the top of a journal page and
beneath it write out your thoughts on how a masterly retreat can be a
victory.

☐ Resolve to fight only for those principles and values that are of lasting
or eternal significance.

☐ Cultivate your role as a peacemaker by creating a strategy for resolving
disputes among your friends.

Things to Remember

Jesus said, "Love your enemies, do good to those who hate you, bless those who curse you, and pray for those who spitefully use you. To him who strikes you on the one cheek, offer the other also. And from him who takes away your cloak, do not withhold your tunic either."

LUKE 6:27–29 NKJV

Repay no one evil for evil. Have regard for good things in the sight of all men. If it is possible, as much as depends on you, live peaceably with all men.

ROMANS 12:17–18 NKJV

Fight the good fight for the Christian faith, take hold of everlasting life, to which you were called and about which you made a good testimony in front of many witnesses.

1 TIMOTHY 6:12 GOD'S WORD

We do not wrestle against flesh and blood, but against principalities, against powers, against the rulers of the darkness of this age, against spiritual hosts of wickedness in the heavenly places.

EPHESIANS 6:12 NKJV

We live in this world, but we don't act like its people.

2 CORINTHIANS 10:3 CEV

Part of the happiness of life consists not in fighting battles, but in avoiding them. A masterly retreat is in itself a victory.

NORMAN VINCENT PEALE

The Jury of Your Peers

Be strong in the Lord and in the power of His might.
—Ephesians 6:10 NKJV

Jenna and Cindi hook up with you after school on a Friday afternoon. Everyone's got only one thing on her mind—it's the weekend! You're all free to do as you please! Jenna tells you that she's going to hang out at Cindi's and later go to McDonald's before heading to the movies. "You want to come?' Cindi asks. You can't, you tell them—your mother asked you to come straight home from school today. They roll their eyes and give each other a knowing look. "That's OK," Jenna says. "We'll see if Teresa can come instead."

Hold it—that's not an example of peer pressure, is it? Nobody pressured you into doing anything. Neither Jenna nor Cindi tried to talk you into going with them. They even said it was OK. So how can this situation have anything to do with peer pressure?

Well, maybe you should take another look, because

these two girls have just pulled off a masterful example of the subtle way teenagers exert pressure on each other. They rolled their eyes ("Here we go again—it's always something"), gave each other a knowing look ("Golly gee, we sure have a sweet little obedient girl here, don't we?"), and said they'd ask Teresa "instead" ("You, child, can be replaced, and don't you forget it!"). They stopped just short of calling you a baby and giving you the boot.

And how about you? Once Jenna and Cindi finished doing their number on you, didn't your mind start to work overtime? *Mom didn't say why she wanted me to come home. It's not like we have plans or anything. And besides, it's Friday, and I should be able to do what I want after being cooped up in school all week. And if they start hanging around with Teresa—well, they know Teresa and I don't get along, so I don't want that to happen...* Do you still think you haven't been pressured?

Peer pressure does not have to be heavy-handed to be effective; it can be as subtle as a brief glance passing between two people. It's an incredibly powerful mechanism for getting you to do what someone else wants you to do. It influences the way you walk and talk and dress and behave and spend your time—as well as who you spend your time with. It's manipulation to the max.

Can you see now what you're up against? It's going to take all the strength and discipline you can muster—and a whole lot of quick and silent prayers—to maintain your resolve to do the right thing when your friends lay a peer-pressure trip on you. You need to be "strong in the Lord and in the power of His might"—all the time, day in and day out. There's just no other way. You can try to resist the pressure in your own strength, but there will come a day when you're tired of always being the one who says no, always trying to do the right thing, and you'll no longer have the strength to walk away. Without God's power to support you, you'll simply give in.

The way to plug in to God's power, and stay plugged in, is to first make sure you have a daily routine that includes spending time with Him, in prayer, in the Word, in meditation and reflection. Then you have to go one step further: You need to put on the whole armor of God—the belt of truth, the shoes of the good news about peace, the shield of faith, the helmet of God's saving power, the sword of the Word of God. (You can find a complete description of this armor in Ephesians 6 in the New Testament.)

Only when you leave the house each morning wearing the armor of God can you hope to be prepared for the pressure you will face. The belt will help you recognize deception. The shoes will remind you to share—and live by—the gospel. The shield will keep doubt at bay. The helmet will assure you of your standing with God. And the sword—your one offensive weapon—will slice through your enemy's cagey attempts to keep you from obeying God. The armor of God is critical—don't leave home without it!

I Will

Put on the armor of God before I leave the house each morning.

yes _____ no _____

Trust God to help me resist the temptation to go along with the crowd.

yes _____ no _____

Learn to recognize both the subtle and overt ways teenagers pressure each other.

yes _____ no _____

Make every effort to avoid placing the wrong kind of pressure on my friends.

yes _____ no _____

Be aware that peer pressure will extend even into my adult years.

yes _____ no _____

Things to Do

☐ Peer pressure existed even in Jesus' time. Read the scriptures that follow to find out who was exerting the pressure.

☐ Memorize Proverbs 4:14–15 and 3 John 1:1.

☐ Thank God in advance for helping you stand strong in the face of peer pressure.

☐ Write a letter to an imaginary (or real) friend who is feeling pressured to do drugs. Explain how he or she can resist the pressure.

☐ Read Ephesians 6:10–18 and come up with a way to remind yourself to put on the whole armor of God each day.

Things to Remember

Do not enter the path of the wicked, and do not walk in the way of evil. Avoid it, do not travel on it; turn away from it and pass on.

PROVERBS 4:14–15 NKJV

Paul wrote: Many live as enemies of the cross of Christ; I have often told you of them, and now I tell you even with tears. Their end is destruction, their god is the belly, and their glory is in their shame; their minds are set on earthly things.

PHILIPPIANS 3:18–19 NRSV

Do not imitate what is evil, but what is good. He who does good is of God, but he who does evil has not seen God.

—3 JOHN 1:11 NKJV

There was much complaining among the people concerning Him. Some said, "He is good"; others said, "No, on the contrary, He deceives the people." However, no one spoke openly of Him for fear of the Jews.

JOHN 7:12–13 NKJV

Nevertheless even among the rulers many believe in Him, but because of the Pharisees they did now confess Him, lest they be put out of the synagogue; for they loved the praise of men more than the praise of God.

JOHN 12:42–43 NKJV

His parents answered them and said, "We know that this is our son, and that he was born blind; but by what means he now sees we do not know . . . He is of age; ask him. He will speak for himself." His parents said these things because they feared the Jews, for the Jews had agreed already that if anyone confessed that He was Christ, he would be put out of the synagogue.

JOHN 9:20–22 NKJV

Pilate sought to release Him, but the Jews cried out, saying, "If you let this Man go, you are not Caesar's friend. Whoever makes himself a king speaks against Caesar." When Pilate therefore heard that saying, he brought Jesus out and sat down in the judgment seat in a place that is called The Pavement, but in Hebrew, Gabbatha.

JOHN 19:12–13 NKJV

The things which you learned and received and heard and saw in me, these do, and the God of peace will be with you.

PHILIPPIANS 4:9 NKJV

I have forgiven that one for your sakes in the presence of Christ, lest Satan should take advantage of us; for we are not ignorant of his devices.

2 CORINTHIANS 2:10–11 NKJV

Character is always lost when a high ideal is sacrificed on the altar of conformity and popularity.

—AUTHOR UNKNOWN

The opposite of bravery is not cowardice but conformity.

—ROBERT ANTHONY

Endless Possibilities

I know the thoughts that I think toward you, says the LORD, thoughts of peace and not of evil, to give you a future and a hope.

—Jeremiah 29:11 NKJV

What do you say when the zillionth person asks what your plans are for the future? Maybe you have a specific goal in life, so your plans naturally line up with that goal; you want to be a doctor, so you know you'll be going to medical school. Perhaps you're not sure exactly what you want to do, but you have several ideas in mind, possibly social work or teaching; either one will require a college degree, so you decide to take some basic courses at first until you can refine your goals. If you're joining the family business, well, your path is pretty obvious to everyone.

Or maybe you're like Nick. He developed an elaborate plan for his life, starting with four years of college and then law school, spending each summer on the mission field. Then he'd marry and wait two years before having children. Nick has overhauled his plan three times since high school, and he's now taking courses at a community college while he figures out what to do with his life!

Making plans for the future is tricky business, that's for sure. You can't predict the future, but you can't ignore it either. And then there's the not-so-small matter of God's will to consider. So where do you start? That depends on whether you want to let God lead or you want to go your own way, hiding your crossed fingers behind your back. If you let God lead, all you have to do is follow. If you go your own way, you have to hope and pray that God will bless your plans and bail you out when things go wrong.

When you allow God to set your course, you lay your future before Him and let Him order your steps. Your willingness to follow Him delights the Father so much that He will give you every opportunity to reach your goal. He'll open doors for you that no one else could open—and He'll close those doors that you should not walk through. He'll give you possibilities for your future that you can't even imagine today.

Meanwhile, what answer can you give your questioner that makes sense in the current economic climate and the future job market and all that? Tell the truth: Your divine Dad is helping you plan your future—and no one knows the future like He does.

I Will

Consult God before making any plans for my life.   _yes_   _no_

Relax in the knowledge that God will not steer me
in the wrong direction.   _yes_   _no_

Learn to recognize the signs that indicate I'm on
the right track.   _yes_   _no_

Be thankful that I have help in sorting
out my future.   _yes_   _no_

Be open to whatever God has in store for me.   _yes_   _no_

Remember that only God knows the future.   _yes_   _no_

Things to Do

☐ Ask God what His plans are for your life.

☐ Listen for His answer.

☐ Memorize Jeremiah 29:11.

☐ Set aside a page in your journal where you can write down those things
that God reveals to you about His plan.

☐ Come up with an appropriate answer to give those who ask about your
plans, and be prepared to gently defend your decision to trust God.

☐ Decide what you can do today that fits in to God's plan for your life.

Things to Remember

Commit your way to the LORD, trust also in Him, and He shall bring it to pass.

PSALM 37:5 NKJV

Jesus said, "When [the shepherd] brings out his own sheep, he goes before them, and the sheep follow him, for they know his voice."

JOHN 10:4 NKJV

Let them do good, that they be rich in good works, ready to give, willing to share, storing up for themselves a good foundation for the time to come, that they may lay hold on eternal life.

1 TIMOTHY 6:18–19 NKJV

There is laid up for me the crown of righteousness, which the Lord, the righteous Judge, will give to me on that Day, and not to me only but also to all who have loved His appearing.

2 TIMOTHY 4:8 NKJV

Plan for this world as if you expect to live forever; but plan for the hereafter as if you expect to die tomorrow.

IBN GABIROL

Expect the best, plan for the worst, and prepare to be surprised.

DENIS WAITLEY

Gray Matters

Your ears shall hear a word behind you, saying, "This is the way, walk in it." Whenever you turn to the right hand or whenever you turn to the left.

—Isaiah 30:21 NKJV

Your parents, who think your schedule is overloaded, give you an ultimatum—give up your spot on the cheerleading squad or quit volunteering at the public library. You love to do both: Cheerleading keeps you physically fit, and working at the library keeps you mentally fit. What should you do?

The youth pastor just posted a list of summer missions opportunities: Help build low-income housing with Habitat for Humanity, assist with Vacation Bible School, join a team sharing the gospel at the beach, or do yard work for disabled people. You would like doing all of these projects, but you'll only have one week off before you start your summer job. Which project will you choose?

Your best friend's parents have just invited you to join their family on a vacation to Mexico. But the trip conflicts with the timing of a special college-level course that would just about seal your admission to the university you want to attend. You can't do both—but both would broaden your experience. How can you possibly decide between the two?

Many choices are easy. Should you do drugs or do God? Watch an X-rated video or walk out of the room? Steal a CD or pay for it? You know the right choice in those situations. But how about when it's not a question of right or wrong, when the options seem more or less equal? You need some solid guidance and a healthy dose of wisdom.

As with everything, the first step you should take is to consult with God. Consider the pros and cons of each option you have, as well as the short- and long-range consequences of your decision. Consider, too, your heart's desire; you can often trust your heart, but only if it is totally surrendered to God. Take into account the seriousness of the situation; in less important situations, one decision may be just as good as another, while other circumstances may require the godly counsel of your parents, teachers, or pastor.

In those gray areas of life, a wrong decision may be uncomfortable but is usually not life-shattering. If you realize you've made the wrong choice, reverse it if possible. Learn from your mistakes. Don't get down on yourself. Think back to the decision-making process you used and revise it the next time you have a tricky choice to make. And always listen for that voice that says, "This is the way, walk in it."

I Will

Consult with God first.

yes ___ no ___

Think carefully about where each choice I make
may take me.

yes ___ no ___

Consider the long- and short-range consequences
of my choices.

yes ___ no ___

Realize that I cannot leave significant decisions
to chance.

yes ___ no ___

Trust my heart only if it is completely
surrendered to God.

yes ___ no ___

Things to Do

☐ Make the best decision: Decide now that you will consult with God first
whenever you're confronted with a major decision.

☐ Read Life on the Edge by James Dobson, a book designed to help teens
make the right choices.

☐ Memorize Isaiah 30:21.

☐ Develop a decision-making strategy for the gray areas in life. Write it
down.

☐ Recall the last time you made a bad decision—a real whopper. See what
you can learn from that situation.

Things to Remember

Trust in the L{\scriptsize ORD} with all your heart, and lean not on your own understanding; in all your ways acknowledge Him, and He shall direct your paths.

PROVERBS 3:5–6 NKJV

I will instruct you and teach you in the way you should go; I will guide you with My eye.

PSALM 32:8 NKJV

The steps of a good man are ordered by the L{\scriptsize ORD}, and He delights in his way.

PSALM 37:23 NKJV

Moses said, "The L{\scriptsize ORD}, He is the One who goes before you. He will be with you, He will not leave you nor forsake you; do not fear nor be dismayed."

DEUTERONOMY 31:8 NKJV

Where there is no counsel, the people fall; but in the multitude of counselors there is safety.

PROVERBS 11:14 NKJV

. . . .

Every choice you make has an end result.

ZIG ZIGLAR

The man or woman who is wholly or joyously surrendered to Christ can't make a wrong choice—any choice will be the right one.

A. W. TOZER

Cutting Loose

Our mouth was filled with laughter, and our tongue with singing. Then they said among the nations, "The LORD has done great things for them." —Psalm 126:2 NKJV

Most people don't have to be reminded to laugh. You probably have genuinely funny friends who come up with such great wisecracks that even the teachers have to laugh. Unless you're telling mean-spirited jokes at someone else's expense, laughter hardly seems to be a spiritual issue. So why talk about "cutting loose"? If anything, people act as if you never take life seriously enough as it is!

Maybe you do need to take life more seriously. Just don't take yourself too seriously in the process. The ability to laugh at yourself—with all your weaknesses and foibles and missteps—gives you a healthy and balanced perspective that will carry you through many awkward situations in your life. When you can make light of an embarrassing performance in which you are the red-faced star, you put everyone at ease, especially yourself. You've probably already witnessed a scenario like that: The principal or the pastor or a guest speaker in an assembly program makes an incredibly stupid mistake. Everyone seems to hold their breath until the "star" cracks a joke about his gaffe. You can actually hear everyone start to breathe again, can't you?

Cutting loose does carry a set of rules, though. Never, ever demean yourself. When you laugh at yourself in a derogatory way, it makes everyone around you uncomfortable, and it diminishes the value that God places on your life. You end up feeling worse than you did when you made the original mistake, which is exactly the opposite of what you're trying to accomplish. You want to feel better about the situation, right? So keep it light, and find the humor in the "humanness" of all those things you do that you think make you look foolish. Realize that they just make you look human.

God gave you the gift of laughter to balance out the problems that will come into your life, just as they come into everyone's life. Look at the older people you know: The ones with a twinkle in their eye are those who have learned to use the gift of laughter wisely. They've developed a sense of humor that lets them take the garbage Satan has tried to dump on them and fling it back in his face. (Imagine how he'd look with rotten leftovers from a broken Hefty bag dripping all over him.)

Delight in the things God intended you to delight in. Make light of your blunders and cherish the joy of laughter. Cut loose—and go live the abundant life.

I Will

Honor God by having a balanced perspective on who I am.

yes _____ no _____

Delight in the life God has given me.

yes _____ no _____

Understand the difference between laughing at myself in a healthy way and degrading myself.

yes _____ no _____

Make light of the mistakes I make.

yes _____ no _____

Put others at ease with my sense of humor.

yes _____ no _____

Refuse to participate in mean-spirited jokes.

yes _____ no _____

Things to Do

☐ Watch your favorite sitcom or comedy and take note of how much of the humor is degrading.

☐ Ask God to make you sensitive to any kind of joking that could hurt someone else.

☐ Read Job 8:1–21 to see how repentance can lead to laughter.

☐ Learn about the health benefits of laughter.

☐ Check out one of the many Christian humor books, like Bible Humor: Top Seven Lists by David Veerman and Rich Anderson.

☐ Visit the Fellowship of Merry Christians at <http://www.joyfulnoiseletter.com/>.

Things to Remember

Jesus said, "Blessed are you who hunger now, for you shall be filled. Blessed are you who weep now, for you shall laugh."

LUKE 6:21 NKJV

Light shines on the godly, and joy on those who do right.

PSALM 97:11 NLT

He will yet fill your mouth with laughing, and your lips with rejoicing.

JOB 8:21 NKJV

A merry heart makes a cheerful countenance, but by sorrow of the heart the spirit is broken.

PROVERBS 15:13 NKJV

And Sarah said, "God has made me laugh, and all who hear will laugh with me."

GENESIS 21:6 NKJV

The LORD said, "Then out of them shall proceed thanksgiving and the voice of those who make merry; I will multiply them, and they shall not diminish; I will also glorify them, and they shall not be small."

JEREMIAH 30:19 NKJV

Hearty laughter is a good way to jog internally without having to go outdoors.

NORMAN COUSINS

Body Language

*Let every man be swift to hear, slow to speak,
slow to wrath.*

—James 1:19 NKJV

You stare at the test you've just been handed and wonder what on earth it's about. Uh-oh. The test is based on what your teacher said in class. Big problem. *Oh, why didn't I take notes?* you think.

You're riding home from church with your parents, and all they can talk about is how great the sermon was. Huh? *What's she talking about?* It sure didn't sound like anything special to you.

Then you get home, and your dad says, "Just once I wish you'd listen to me and quit leaving your stuff all over the house." *What's he talking about?* you wonder.

Good listening skills don't seem to come naturally, do they? How can you activate your hearing?

Listen with your hands. Get in the habit of taking notes. As you go through life, you'll discover that even once you're out of school—whether high school or college—you'll find yourself in countless situations that require note-taking.

Listen with your spirit. Expect God to speak to you every time you hear a sermon, a testimony, a Christian television or radio program, or a Christian CD. You can activate your spirit by asking God to reveal to you what He wants you to get out of the message, and that in turn activates your hearing.

Listen with your actions. Productive listening requires action. When your dad says he wishes you'd listen to him, he means he wants you to obey him—not just hear his words accurately. The same principle holds for spiritual listening. James 1:22 tells believers to be "doers of the word, and not hearers only."

Listen with your mouth. It's been said that God gave you two ears and one mouth because He wants you to listen twice as much as you talk. But you can "listen" by asking the right questions at the right time.

Listen with your eyes. In every situation, you'd do well to discipline yourself to look at the person speaking to you. That goes for your teacher, your pastor, your parents, and anyone you have a conversation with.

Above all, learn to look at God when He speaks to you. Keep your focus on Him. Let Him know that you care about what He's saying to you, that you not only believe Him and believe in Him but you also have every intention of acting on what He tells you to do. Then go out and do it.

I Will

Expect God to speak to me.   _yes_   _no_

Show my love for God by giving Him my
wholehearted attention.   _yes_   _no_

Make sure that I am a doer of the Word and not just
a hearer.   _yes_   _no_

Learn what it means to activate my hearing.   _yes_   _no_

Listen twice as much as I speak.   _yes_   _no_

Show respect by paying attention when
someone is talking.   _yes_   _no_

Things to Do

☐ Ask God to speak to you through a message given by your pastor or youth leader.

☐ Take notes during the next sermon you hear. If you're already in the habit, try to take better notes.

☐ Learn to recognize "action points"—practical things you can do—by consciously listening for them the next time you hear a sermon or other message.

☐ Make a commitment to God that you will do what you have heard Him tell you to do.

☐ Pay close attention to the way people listen to you tomorrow. Write down what you appreciated and what annoyed you about their behavior.

Things to Remember

Jesus said to them, "He who has ears to hear, let him hear!"

MARK 4:9 NKJV

Jesus said, "He who has an ear, let him hear what the Spirit says to the churches."

REVELATION 2:29 NKJV

Moses said, "Because you have listened to the voice of the LORD your God, to keep all His commandments which I command you today, to do what is right in the eyes of the LORD your God."

DEUTERONOMY 13:18 NKJV

David wrote: Come, you children, listen to me; I will teach you the fear of the LORD.

PSALM 34:11 NKJV

The LORD said, "Oh, that My people would listen to Me, that Israel would walk in My ways!"

PSALM 81:13 NKJV

• •

Listening, not imitation, may be the sincerest form of flattery.

JOYCE BROTHERS

The greatest gift you can give another is the purity of your attention.

RICHARD MOSS

Who's the Boss?

> Whatever you do, do it heartily, as to the Lord and not to men, knowing that from the Lord you will receive the reward of the inheritance; for you serve the Lord Christ.
> —Colossians 3:23–24 NKJV

Say you come home from school one day and there's no food in the house—nothing at all. You think, *This is it. I'm going to die, right here and now. I'm starving!* Physical weakness begins to overtake you. You lie on the sofa, stricken by the fate that has befallen you. All this, and you've only been home for twenty minutes.

You hear your mom's van pull in the driveway, and hope begins to stir deep within you. She must have gone to the supermarket. You look out the window—it's even better than that! She's carrying two huge pizza boxes, and your kid sister is carrying a third box. "Sorry, Son," your mother says, as you lunge toward one of the boxes before they can even get in the house. "You can't have any."

What? What?? Calmly, she quotes the end of 2 Thessalonians 3:10: "If anyone will not work, neither shall he eat." *Gulp*. She nailed you, and nailed you good. All week she had been asking you to help with one thing or another, but you kept putting her off. Last weekend she and your sister cleaned out the garage while you holed up in your room. Unfortunately, your behavior over the past week was not unusual—you always seem to find some excuse to get out of helping.

Looks like your day of reckoning has come. If you want to eat again, you'd better get to work. And you'd better get used to the reality that work is not an option, because that's a fact you'll be living with for the rest of your days on earth.

The Bible is very clear about the importance of work—so clear that it calls a person who refuses to work a whole host of crummy names, especially in the book of Proverbs. God designed people to be productive, and He designed work to be an essential factor in shaping a person's life. Your satisfaction in life is so closely tied to the work you do—to your contribution to your family and the community—that the stronger your work ethic is, the more content you'll be.

Maybe you find that hard to swallow right now; work is a four-letter word that you've managed to avoid. Meanwhile, your helpful little sister, Mom's willing worker, finds it pretty easy to swallow, right along with a couple of slices of pepperoni pizza. With extra cheese. And sausage.

I Will

Understand that God designed me to be a productive person.

yes   *no*

Ask God to make me a willing worker.

yes   *no*

Pitch in and help around the house.

yes   *no*

Realize that work is not an option in life.

yes   *no*

View work as a factor in shaping my life and providing lifelong satisfaction.

yes   *no*

Develop a strong work ethic.

yes   *no*

Things to Do

☐ Read through the book of Proverbs, listing all the verses that refer to work or idleness, for an indication of how seriously God views work.

☐ Ask God to show you how you can become a more willing worker.

☐ Make a list of little and big things that you know need to be done around the house. Commit yourself to helping to get those jobs done.

☐ Memorize Colossians 3:23–24 and remember it the next time you have a job to do.

☐ Pretend that you own a business—something you're familiar with, like a retail store. Write down the qualities you'd like in an employee. Concentrate on developing those qualities in your own character.

Things to Remember

Let the beauty of the LORD our God be upon us, and establish the work of our hands for us; yes, establish the work of our hands.

PSALM 90:17 NKJV

Nothing is better for a man than that he should eat and drink, and that his soul should enjoy good in his labor. This also, I saw, was from the hand of God.

ECCLESIASTES 2:24 NKJV

Even when we were with you, we commanded you this: If anyone will not work, neither shall he eat.

2 THESSALONIANS 3:10 NKJV

Let him who stole steal no longer, but rather let him labor, working with his hands what is good, that he may have something to give him who has need.

EPHESIANS 4:28 NKJV

Jesus said to His disciples, "The harvest truly is plentiful, but the laborers are few. Therefore pray the Lord of the harvest to send out laborers into His harvest."

MATTHEW 9:37–38 NKJV

Work for the fun of it, and the money will arrive some day.

RONNIE MILSAP

In case of doubt, do a little more than you have to.

WARREN MITCHELL

The Real Thing

As the deer pants for the water brooks, so pants my soul for You, O God.

—Psalm 42:1 NKJV

A woman you know considers herself a highly spiritual person. She meditates and chants and does some sort of thing with crystals and believes in the healing power of a rock. Meanwhile, the witch down the block—no, not some mean old crab but a real, live, bona fide witch—claims to have found true spirituality in wicca. Your whole family is born-again, and that's supposed to make them spiritual. What gives? How can they all believe they're spiritual?

Spirituality involves those things that nurture your spirit. Because you are a spiritual being, you need to "feed" your spirit in order to be spiritually strong, just as you need to feed your body in order to have physical strength. As a Christian, you've no doubt discovered that the only real way to find true spirituality is through reading the Word of God and cultivating an intimate relationship with the Father through Jesus Christ. In fact, genuine spirituality simply means becoming more Christlike by spending time in His presence.

Other people, like the rock-healer and the witch, often recognize their spiritual nature and sense the need to nurture it. Some openly reject Christ and turn to other gods, but many seek fulfillment in a variety of rituals and philosophies and beliefs only because they've never heard about Jesus—or because what they've heard bears little resemblance to the truth. The apostle Paul understood the spiritual nature of those who worshiped other gods and looked for love in all the wrong places. Instead of criticizing them, he appealed to their spirituality and opened their eyes to the reality of the one true God. Society today is a lot like it was in Paul's day, with so many varieties of religious belief. If you want to be an effective witness, you'd do well to follow Paul's example by acknowledging—and respecting—the spiritual need that causes people to seek other gods in the first place.

If you have had a life-changing encounter with Jesus, you know the hunger deep down inside of you that wants more of Him and less of you. You can try to ignore the hunger by filling up with empty activities, but the hunger never disappears. Nurture your spirit by getting closer to God. Immerse yourself in His presence. Seek to be more Christlike. Fill your mind and heart with God's Word. Your spiritual strength will witness to those whose hunger has yet to lead them to the real thing—Jesus Christ.

I Will

Trust God to keep me from being deceived by
false spirituality.   yes   no

Nurture my spirit by spending time with God and
His Word.   yes   no

Place a high priority on building up my spiritual
strength.   yes   no

Seek to become more Christlike.   yes   no

Acknowledge the spirituality in those who do not
believe as I do.   yes   no

Things to Do

☐ Make it your number one goal to become more Christlike. Write it down, date it, and sign it.

☐ Read how Paul appealed to the spirituality of unbelievers in Acts 17:23–27.

☐ List the varieties of belief that you've encountered in your community. Use Paul's example to create a script to lead adherents of those beliefs to Christ.

☐ Come up with a daily "meal plan" for nurturing your spirit (such as a certain number of "helpings" of prayer, Bible verses, and so forth).

☐ Ask God to keep you from trying to satisfy your spiritual hunger with empty activities.

Things to Remember

On the last day, that great day of the feast, Jesus stood and cried out, saying, "If anyone thirsts, let him come to Me and drink. He who believes in Me, as the Scripture has said, out of his heart will flow rivers of living water."

JOHN 7:37–38 NKJV

Jesus said, "'You shall love the Lord your God with all your heart, with all your soul, with all your mind, and with all your strength.' This is the first commandment."

MARK 12:30 NKJV

Jesus said, "The thief does not come except to steal, and to kill, and to destroy. I have come that they may have life, and that they may have it more abundantly."

JOHN 10:10 NKJV

Oh, taste and see that the LORD is good; blessed is the man who trusts in Him.

PSALM 34:8 NKJV

You are not a human being in search of a spiritual experience. You are a spiritual being immersed in a human experience.

PIERRE TEILHARD DE CHARDIN

When you examine the lives of the most influential people who have ever walked among us, you discover one thread that winds through them all. They have been aligned first with their spiritual nature and only then with their physical selves.

ALBERT EINSTEIN

Turning Down the Noise

My soul, wait silently for God alone, for my expectation is from Him.

—Psalm 62:5 NKJV

What's your idea of a great vacation? A week at Walt Disney World? Surfing in Maui? Rock climbing in the Arizona canyons? How about going to a secluded spot to meditate in complete silence and solitude? Hmm. That last one doesn't sound like much of a vacation. A cross-country road trip with your whole family sounds more appealing. OK, how about a compromise: a ten-minute minivacation—just you and God and whatever thoughts come to mind. No music. No talking. You can do anything for ten minutes, can't you?

Spending time alone with God rejuvenates you and refreshes your spirit. But while some people relish the opportunity to take a spiritual time-out, others find the very thought to be maddening. If you're in the latter category, you'll need to start out by taking a baby step, like a ten-minute minivacation. Before you even attempt that, however, you need to understand what this "vacation" is all about.

Unlike other vacations, a spiritual time-out—a period of silence and solitude in the presence of God—is not an escape from reality. Neither is it a time of idleness and inactivity. It's a break from routine that sharpens your spiritual sensitivity, restores your soul, and energizes you to return to your routine, because you've been drawing on God's power instead of trying to continue on your own.

God's voice becomes clearer to you in an atmosphere of silence and solitude, since His is the only voice you hear. There's also an easily overlooked bonus in spending quiet time with God: You get to know yourself better. That may not seem like much of a bonus, especially if your self-esteem is a bit on the low side. As you become more intimately acquainted with who you are when no one else is around, however, you may be surprised to discover how delightful it is to spend time in your own company! Maybe you don't want to face the real you, or perhaps you are frightened by the negative thoughts and memories that seem to plague you whenever you turn down the noise in your life. If that's the case, it would be helpful for you to realize that facing your fears will only get harder the longer you put it off.

Remember this: God is with you, ready to replace your fears with His peace. As you steadily increase the time you spend in solitude and silence, you may find it hard to remember why you thought Walt Disney World was so great.

I Will

Draw on God's power by taking a spiritual time-out.

yes _no_

Appreciate the benefit of spending time in silence and solitude.

yes _no_

Expect to hear God's voice more clearly as I turn down the noise in my life.

yes _no_

Give God my fear of facing myself and my negative memories.

yes _no_

Become comfortable with spending time by myself.

yes _no_

Things to Do

☐ Go on a minivacation with God—for a few minutes or a few hours.

☐ Seek out a special place in your home or in your neighborhood where you find it easiest to enter God's presence.

☐ Set a timer for thirty minutes. Sit in silence until the time is up. Reflect on the thoughts that come to you.

☐ Ask God what He wants you to learn from your time alone with Him.

☐ Take a walk by yourself. Let your mind wander. Notice where your feet and your thoughts take you.

☐ In your journal, write about how it feels to be alone. Give God any fears that surface.

Things to Remember

Surely I have calmed and quieted my soul, like a weaned child with his mother, like a weaned child my soul is within me.

PSALM 131:2 NKJV

For everything there is a season, and a time for every matter under heaven... a time to tear, and a time to sew; a time to keep silence, and a time to speak.

ECCLESIASTES 3:1, 7 NRSV

It is good that one should hope and wait quietly for the salvation of the LORD.

LAMENTATIONS 3:26 NKJV

We urge you, brethren, that you... aspire to lead a quiet life, to mind your own business, and to work with your own hands, as we commanded you.

1 THESSALONIANS 4:10–11 NKJV

My people will dwell in a peaceful habitation, in secure dwellings, and in quiet resting places.

ISAIAH 32:18 NKJV

•••

The mark of solitude is silence, as speech is the mark of community. Silence and speech have the same inner correspondence and difference as do solitude and community. One does not exist without the other. Right speech comes out of silence, and right silence comes out of speech.

DIETRICH BONHOEFFER

Mastermind

Those who are Christ's have crucified the flesh with its passions and desires.

—Galatians 5:24 NKJV

Crucify the flesh? Did you really read the verse above? You know what crucifixion is, and you know it isn't pretty. What's more, it's a killer. So now the Bible is telling you to kill your body? If that's what you think that means, then you need to understand what the Bible means when it refers to "the flesh." Your flesh is that part of you that gives rise to sinful "passions and desires," as Paul wrote to the Galatians. Your flesh is in a constant battle with your spirit, the part of you that strives to live in a godly way.

If you belong to Christ, your flesh has already been crucified—so avoiding sin should be a piece of cake, right? No, because you still have to deal with Satan, who tries to break down your self-control by becoming the master of your mind, knowing that your thoughts determine your actions. The Bible depicts him as one sneaky creature, prowling about, looking to devour weak believers. Remember, too, that just because he doesn't get you on the "big" sins, that doesn't mean he's defeated. You also need to crucify the flesh by exercising control over any bad habit you have, whether it's eating too many snack cakes or talking on the phone too much or passing notes in class.

You continue to crucify the flesh as you set your mind on the things of the Spirit. You won't be walking around like some haloed saint in a medieval painting, but your awareness of God will become so acute that you will want to do His will instead of satisfying your own desires. You can discipline your body, mind, and spirit to bring honor to His name by not giving in to sinful desire or seemingly innocent addictions, like absolutely having to watch every episode of Friends or buying every teen magazine that even briefly mentions 'N Sync. As one of the nine qualities known as the fruit of the Spirit, self-control shows others that you are a Spirit-controlled believer.

Each time you exercise self-control you grow stronger in the Lord and become more confident in your ability to ward off Satan's future efforts at devouring you. Each time you exercise self-control you also invite peace to settle over your life as you avoid the guilt that comes from knowing you've given in to wrong. Finally, each time you exercise self-control you confirm the high regard you place on maintaining a right relationship with the Father—and that pleases Him to no end.

I Will

Be thankful for the trust God has in me to do the right thing.

     yes   no

Rely on God to help me control myself.

     yes   no

Learn to see the valuable outcome of discipline, no matter how painful it is.

     yes   no

Be aware of the need to control habitual problems (such as excessive phone use).

     yes   no

Avoid people and circumstances that I know tend to weaken my resistance to wrongdoing.

     yes   no

Things to Do

☐ Meditate on what it means to crucify the flesh.

☐ Think of a time when you were most disciplined, such as when you were training for a sport or taking music or dance lessons. Apply the principles you learned then to your personal life now.

☐ Determine your greatest area of indulgence (such as eating). Ask God to help you control that one area for the next week.

☐ Keep a record of your progress for a week.

☐ List concrete objects that represent areas you need to control (like a television or computer). Put each one in its place by announcing that you are superior to it and from now on, you're in control.

Things to Remember

Be on your guard and stay awake. Your enemy, the devil, is like a roaring lion, sneaking around to find someone to attack.

1 PETER 5:8 CEV

No discipline is enjoyable while it is happening—it is painful! But afterward there will be a quiet harvest of right living for those who are trained in this way.

HEBREWS 12:11 NLT

God wants us to turn from godless living and sinful pleasures and to live good, God-fearing lives day after day.

TITUS 2:12 TLB

I will set nothing wicked before my eyes; I hate the work of those who fall away; it shall not cling to me.

PSALM 101:3 NKJV

For this very reason, giving all diligence, add to your faith virtue, to virtue knowledge, to knowledge self-control, to self-control perseverance, to perseverance godliness, to godliness brotherly kindness, and to brotherly kindness love.

2 PETER 1:5-7 NKJV

Such power there is in clear-eyed self-restraint.

JAMES RUSSELL LOWELL

He who reigns within himself and rules passions, desires, and fears is more than a king.

JOHN MILTON

"Now Be Nice"

> As the elect of God, holy and beloved, put on tender
> mercies, kindness, humility, meekness, longsuffering.
> —Colossians 3:12 NKJV

Don't you wish you had a dollar for every time your mother told you to be nice? Hopefully, she doesn't have to say that to you anymore, but you probably heard it a lot when you were younger—especially on your way to visit relatives. Now that you're older, you might wonder about this whole "nice" business, and with good reason: God never tells you to be nice. He tells you to be kind. And the difference between the two is subtle but significant.

Nice is polite; kind is caring, compassionate, and considerate. Nice is superficial; kind is deep, intense, and profound. Kindness is a condition of the heart; a kind person never has to be told, "Now be kind." Compassion is so much a part of their nature that they simply cannot turn away from a person who is suffering. Like Mother Teresa, they see Jesus in every person they meet. To reject any human being is to reject God Himself.

Becoming a compassionate person is not something you can accomplish by following a well-ordered plan. It stems from a deep and abiding understanding of the compassion Jesus felt for those who were crying out for a Savior—the One who could heal them of diseases, deliver them from demons, and lead them from deception. Needy, helpless people surrounded Him and followed Him wherever He went. His deep love for them moved Him to not only meet their needs but also to empower His disciples to continue His work after He returned to the Father. And He promises to impart to you His love for suffering people just as He imparted it to the disciples.

As your heart fills with compassion, you will become more aware than ever of the tremendous need in the people around you. Keep in mind that it's not just the poor, the hungry, and the homeless who could use a strong dose of the love of Jesus. It's anyone who is hurting or needy, for any reason at all. Could you become the eyes for an elderly woman who is losing her sight? A big sister to an at-risk child who is fresh out of role models? A mechanic for a single mother whose car balks at getting her to work every day?

The simplest act of kindness becomes an extraordinary blessing when God's Spirit is involved. Allow His Spirit to move your heart with compassion, and then follow His lead. Your actions could very well have eternal consequences.

I Will

Meditate on the love and compassion Jesus had
for the suffering people around Him. _yes_ _no_

Be sensitive to the needs of people I know as well
as people around the world. _yes_ _no_

Exchange my niceness for a genuine and healthy
helping of compassion. _yes_ _no_

See Jesus in every person I meet. _yes_ _no_

Be agreeable, sympathetic, and empathetic toward
others. _yes_ _no_

Things to Do

☐ Read the story of the Good Samaritan in Luke 10:30–37.

☐ Ask God to fill your heart with compassion.

☐ Find out more about the work Mother Teresa did in India—and what
kept her going in the midst of horrible and unfathomable circumstances.

☐ List some things you could do as anonymous acts of kindness for
people in your community.

☐ Make a list of people in your school and church who could benefit from
your help.

☐ Read Burn by Brian Shipman, a book for teens about compassion.

Things to Remember

Pure and undefiled religion before God and the Father is this: to visit orphans and widows in their trouble, and to keep oneself unspotted from the world.

JAMES 1:27 NKJV

By purity, by knowledge, by longsuffering, by kindness, by the Holy Spirit, by sincere love.

2 CORINTHIANS 6:6 NKJV

When He saw the multitudes, He was moved with compassion for them, because they were weary and scattered, like sheep having no shepherd.

MATTHEW 9:36 NKJV

The fruit of the Spirit is love, joy, peace, longsuffering, kindness, goodness, faithfulness, gentleness, self-control. Against such there is no law.

GALATIANS 5:22–23 NKJV

Be kind to one another, tenderhearted, forgiving one another, even as God in Christ forgave you.

EPHESIANS 4:32 NKJV

· ·

Man may dismiss compassion from his heart, but God never will.

WILLIAM COWPER

Biblical orthodoxy without compassion is surely the ugliest thing in the world.

FRANCIS SCHAEFFER

All Grown Up

Let us go on to perfection, not laying again the foundation of repentance from dead works and of faith toward God.
—*Hebrews 6:1 NKJV*

This is it. Your moment has arrived. It's time to move on, to leave your adolescence behind and accept the responsibility that everyone has told you will come. How will you know that this is your day? Will you rely on the government's assessment? The state may declare you an adult at age eighteen, granting you a dazzling array of rights and privileges. But does that mean that you're now mature—or perfect, as some Bible versions translate the word? No way.

The day you recognize the need to accept responsibility for your life is the day you take your single biggest step toward maturity. You can do that right now, regardless of your age. Start with some very practical steps, like assuming responsibility for doing your own laundry or cleaning up after yourself when you take a shower or have a snack. Keep track of your own appointments. Give your parents plenty of notice when you need to buy something extra for school or you need a ride somewhere. These are small steps, but they can make a big difference.

There are other areas in your life in which you can actively work your way toward greater maturity. You already know one way: taking responsibility for your own actions and words. You can also take specific steps that will help you mature spiritually. Do you have a solid grounding in the basics of your faith? Then it's time to go on to some serious Bible study. It's also time to go deeper in prayer, trusting God to do above and beyond what you can even imagine. How about evangelism? Are you ready to take on more responsibility for sharing the gospel with others? Then there's teaching—can you help teach young children in a Sunday school class? Maybe it's time for you to start a Christian group at school or organize a special youth rally for Christ.

All these actions will help you mature in your faith, because each one requires a deeper dependency on God. You cannot expect to succeed when you take on this kind of responsibility unless you rely on God. Every spiritual activity you perform is another brick in the building of faith that you are creating.

You can keep on adding years to your age without ever moving an inch toward maturity. Or you can gradually take on more responsibility and in the process mature well beyond your years. Which will it be?

I Will

Expect God to help me as I take each step toward
greater maturity.   yes _____   no _____

Recognize the need to accept responsibility
for my life.   yes _____   no _____

Take on more responsibilities at home.   yes _____   no _____

Realize that my age has nothing to do with
my maturity.   yes _____   no _____

Actively work toward maturing spiritually.   yes _____   no _____

Learn to rely on God for increasingly bigger things.   yes _____   no _____

Things to Do

☐ Write in your journal about the relationship between responsibility and
maturity.

☐ Make a commitment to gradually accept more responsibility in all areas
of your life.

☐ Choose one task, such as doing your own laundry, that you can take on
immediately.

☐ Seek suggestions from your pastor or youth leader for a meaty Bible
study that would be appropriate for you.

☐ Find out how you can help out with the younger children at church.

Things to Remember

Do not be children in understanding; however, in malice, be babes, but in understanding be mature.

1 CORINTHIANS 14:20 NKJV

Everyone who partakes only of milk is unskilled in the word of righteousness, for he is a babe. But solid food belongs to those who are of full age, that is, those who by reason of use have their senses exercised to discern both good and evil.

HEBREWS 5:13–14 NKJV

Till we all come to the unity of the faith and of the knowledge of the Son of God, to a perfect man, to the measure of the stature of the fullness of Christ; that we should no longer be children, tossed to and fro and carried about with every wind of doctrine, by the trickery of men, in the cunning craftiness of deceitful plotting.

EPHESIANS 4:13–14 NKJV

Him we preach, warning every man and teaching every man in all wisdom, that we may present every man perfect in Christ Jesus.

COLOSSIANS 1:28 NKJV

In the last analysis, the individual person is responsible for living his own life and for "finding himself." If he persists in shifting his responsibility to somebody else, he fails to find out the meaning of his own existence.

THOMAS MERTON

Other Books in the Checklist for Life Series

Checklist for Life
ISBN 0-7852-6455-8

Checklist for Life for Women
ISBN 0-7852-6462-0

Checklist for Life for Men
ISBN 0-7852-6463-9